BERNARD SEAL

A·M·E·R·I·C·A·N

VOCABULARY BUILDER 2

Longman

American Vocabulary Builder 2
Adaptation of Vocabulary Builder 2, by Bernard Seal
Published by Longman Group Limited, 1987

Longman, 10 Bank Street, White Plains, N.Y. 10606

Associated companies:
Longman Group Ltd., London
Longman Cheshire Pty., Melbourne
Longman Paul Pty., Auckland
Copp Clark Pitman, Toronto

Distributed in the United Kingdom by Longman Group
Ltd., Longman House, Burnt Mill, Harlow, Essex CM20
2JE, England and by associated companies, branches,
and representatives throughout the world.

ISBN 0-8013-0536-5

5 6 7 8 9 10-HC-99989796959493

Contents

Introduction   4   Acknowledgments   7

■■■

Section 1: At home

1.1   Parts of the house   8   **1.6**   Cooking   20

1.2   Furniture and furnishings   10   **1.7**   Eating   22

1.3   Sleeping   12   **1.8**   Keeping food fresh   24

1.4   Washing   14   **1.9**   Clothes   26

1.5   Housework   16   **1.10**   Fashions   28

      Review   18   *Review*   30

■■■

Section 2: At play

2.1   Sports   32   **2.6**   Entertainers   44

2.2   Actions in sports   34   **2.7**   Music   46

2.3   Party time   36   **2.8**   Television   48

2.4   Places to go and things to do   38   **2.9**   Reading   50

2.5   Time for a laugh   40   **2.10**   The art of conversation   52

      Review   42   *Review*   54

■■■

Section 3: At work

3.1   Jobs   56   **3.6**   Education   68

3.2   Farm work   58   **3.7**   Medical matters   70

3.3   Tools and their uses   60   **3.8**   The law   72

3.4   Shopping   62   **3.9**   Politics   74

3.5   Money   64   **3.10**   Space   76

      Review   66   *Review*   78

■■■

Index   80   Key   85

Introduction

To the student

This book is intended to help you expand your vocabulary. It is written for students who are approaching the intermediate level. While studying *Vocabulary Builder 2*, it is a good idea for you to use a dictionary for intermediate learners of English, such as the *Longman Active Study Dictionary*.

Vocabulary Builder 2 is divided into three sections: **At home, At play** and **At work**. Each section has ten units that deal with different groups of words, and each unit contains several parts.

The first part is called **Words in context** and contains a passage or passages for you to read and study. You should try to read these passages without a dictionary. The key words are in dark print and in most cases you should be able to guess the meanings of these words from the way they are used in the passage. If you are not sure of the meaning of a word, always look back at the sentence before and after it. These sentences will often help to explain the word. You should also have a general idea of the meaning, because all the key words are closely related. For example, the first unit is called **Parts of the house** and all the key words (kitchen, fence, stairs, hall, basement, etc.) are all connected in some way to houses. This should help you guess the meanings of any words that you don't know.

Exercise 1 follows the **Words in context** passage. This is a reading comprehension exercise. In many cases the questions focus on the meanings of the key words.

Exercise 2 and **Exercise 3** test your knowledge of the key words in the passage. Before you do these exercises you should always look back at the passage and see how the key words have been used.

Each unit also has a fourth exercise called either **Dictionary work** or **Just for fun**. The **Dictionary work** exercise introduces more vocabulary related to the subject of the unit. You will usually need a dictionary for this exercise because you do not have a passage to help you guess the meaning of the words. The **Just for fun** exercises give you a chance to have some fun with the words you have been studying. For some of these exercises, it will be helpful if you can talk to someone who is also studying English so that you can share your ideas.

The final section, **Think about**, is also best done with a friend. It should help you to use the words in an interesting discussion.

You can study the units in any order you like, but it is best to study them in groups of five(e.g. units 1.1–1.5 or 2.6–2.10). Then, at the end of each five units, you can review the words you have studied in the **Vocabulary review** section. You can then also test your knowledge of these words in one of the six **Test yourself** exercises.

There is also an **Index** of key words at the back of the book which includes a phonetic guide to pronunciation. The **Index** gives the number of each unit in which the word appears.

To the teacher

Vocabulary Builder 2 can be used either as classroom material or as self-study material for pre-intermediate to intermediate students who want to build their vocabulary.

The approach

Vocabulary Builder 2 present key words in lexical sets embedded in texts. The meanings of the items can often be guessed from their context, and knowledge of the words is extended, practiced and tested in a series of exercises.

Each book is divided into three large subject areas, containing ten units. Each unit teaches a lexical set, such as different housecleaning chores, adjectives used in describing food, types of television programs, or ways of describing your health. There are two principal reasons for teaching vocabulary in sets. First, students often feel that they learn vocabulary in a somewhat random way. Putting the words into lexical sets makes their study more structured. Each unit studied then gives a sense of measurable progress. Secondly, since all the words in a lexical set are related, the student has an immediate clue as to the meaning of a previously unknown word. Thus, for example, when encountering the word "shoot" in the unit "Actions in sports" the student will realize that it is something that a sportsperson does while playing a sport.

Each lexical set is presented in a reading passage or passages at the beginning of a unit. These passages may seem difficult. The syntax and structures in them have not been tightly controlled and you may well feel that the language is beyond the productive capabilities of your students. This has been done intentionally. The aim is to have students reading at a level that stretches and challenges them, provided that they are able to maintain a general sense of what the text is about.

The passages have been carefully written so that the more difficult lexical items can be guessed from the context in which they occur. This may often involve a certain degree of textual redundancy which enables the meaning of the target items to be made clearer by the extra clues. Given these clues, the students learn to guess the meanings of words from their contexts and are encouraged not to become too dependent on the dictionary while they are reading. It is important that students develop good reading habits. They should learn to read fluently, tolerating a certain degree of ambiguity while maintaining an interest in the gist of the passage.

The target words are clearly marked in a bold typeface on their first occurrence in the text. Each target item occurs again in at least one of the exercises that follow. These exercises are designed to reinforce the meanings of the target words and to test the students' understanding of how they should be used. The fact that each target item appears in bold print enables the students to return to the original **Words in context** passage to find an example of its usage. This will help them do the exercises.

Contents of a unit
● *Words in context*
A short passage or passages containing the target words in the lexical set.

● *Exercise 1*

A comprehension exercise that leads students to understand the overall meaning of the passage and at the same time focuses attention on some of the key vocabulary items.

● *Exercises 2 and 3*

Each of the target lexical items is encountered in at least one of these exercises. The exercises are designed to extend the students' understanding of the items.

● *Dictionary work/Just for fun*

Dictionary work exercises encourage students to expand their vocabulary by introducing a lexical set related to the topic of the unit. The students will usually need a dictionary to complete these exercises.

Just for fun exercises may take various forms: ranking and rating exercises, games, and other communicative activities. These exercises are intended to further the students' interest in the topic and to give them an opportunity to use some of the target lexical items in a stress-free context.

● *Think about*

These are discussion questions, designed to activate the students' production of the target words in a conversation or discussion.

How to use Vocabulary Builder 2 in the classroom

Each unit is designed so that it can form the basis for a one-hour lesson. However, the material should be flexible enough to be used in parts over a series of lessons if preferred. Teachers may also find that they can use the book to combine in-class work with self-study.

One of the main aims of the *Vocabulary Builder 2* is to promote a problem-solving approach to vocabulary learning. On their first encounter with the target items in the reading passages, students are expected to try to work out the meanings without much teacher guidance and without the use of a dictionary. Be aware, therefore, that too much pre-teaching will destroy the point of the exercises. It is suggested that you introduce the topic of the unit with some brief pre-questions relating to the topic. Then, if you want to pre-teach some vocabulary items, only pre-teach those words that you feel will facilitate your students' understanding of the text, but which are not key words (i.e. words that do not appear in bold print in the text).

The first time you use the book, you should explain to the students why you do not want them to use a dictionary when studying the passages. Point out how many of the difficult words can be guessed from their context. This can be illustrated by taking one of the passages and going through it with the class. The students will soon get used to searching for the context clues and doing without a dictionary.

Let your students work silently once they start reading the passage. When they are ready, they should attempt to answer the questions in **Exercise 1**. Encourage students to share their answers in pairs.

At this stage (when all the students have read the passage and attempted **Exercise 1**) you may want to read the passage aloud so they can hear how the words are pronounced. Your phrasing may also help the students to understand the passage better. It is best if you wait until they have read through the passage silently before they hear it, because this promotes the habit of silent reading when they are on their own.

Exercise 2 and **Exercise 3** may then be done as whole-class or pair-work activities or individually, whichever seems more appropriate. In general, easier exercises should be done individually, with the students checking their answers with their neighbours, and more difficult problem-solving exercises should be done in pairs or small groups.

Just for fun exercises are designed for work in pairs or small groups. Make sure the students are absolutely clear about what they have to do in their groups. This should be a relaxed, active and enjoyable phase of the lesson.

Dictionary work exercises may either be done in class with dictionaries or as homework.

The **Think about** questions are intended to get students talking and using the vocabulary of the lesson. There are only a few discussion questions in each unit so you may wish to add some of your own.

There are twenty-five test sentences in each **Test yourself** section: five for each of the previous five units. Having completed one unit, you may, therefore, want to set your students the task of finding and answering the five sentences in the **Test yourself** section that test the use of five of the key words in that unit. Alternatively, to make most effective use of the **Test yourself** sections, teach the units in groups of five, (i.e. units 1.1 to 1.5 or 2.6 to 2.10). Then let your students complete the **Test yourself** section.

It is possible to teach the units in any order. They have not been sequenced in difficulty and do not rely on the students having studied one unit in order to study the next.

Acknowledgments

To those who use this book it may seem as though such a small and simple book could not have required too much pain and effort. Be undeceived. Many hours of work, many revisions, much testing and a great deal of discussion have gone into the creation of these few pages.

Many people at Longman have made substantial contributions, in particular, Malcolm Booker, Susan Maingay, Della Summers and Deborah Tricker. As usual, the English Language Centre in Hove, Sussex, has provided me with essential facilities. Special thanks to Dr. Ian Dunlop, Norma Williams and Dave Brown. Colleagues, too, at the American Language Institute at the University of Southern California have helped by testing materials and giving much needed moral support. Thanks, also, are due to Robert O'Neill for valuable input in the developmental stages of the project.

Finally, let me acknowledge the contribution of my wife, Chris, who, being an ESL teacher herself, has not only helped with ideas, tested materials, and suggested changes, but has also had to fortify me during some of the more frustrating moments of getting the book completed.

1 At home

1.1 Parts of the house

Words in context

Read the following passage and do the exercises.

Mr. Hernandez sells houses. At the moment he is showing 736 Pearblossom Avenue to Mr. and Mrs. Willis.

"Here we are. As you can see, Mr. and Mrs. Willis, it's really quite a big house, with two **stories. Upstairs** there are three **bedrooms** and a **bathroom**, and **downstairs** we have a large **living room**, a **dining room**, and a **kitchen**. There is no **basement** under the house.

"Before we go in, let's take a look at the house from the outside. I think you'll agree that the **front yard** is a nice size and the **hedge** around it makes it a little more private. There's a two-car **garage** next to the house, and, as you can see, the **driveway** is in very good condition. Now, look up there at the **roof**. It was repaired only four months ago, so you won't have any trouble from the rain. As you can see, there's a **chimney** up there. The house has a working **fireplace**. And the present owners put in a new **furnace**, so you'll have plenty of heat all winter.

"O.K. Let's go in here through the front **gate** and up the **walk** to the **front door**. Follow me.

"I'll just open the door and here we are inside. Here's a little **hall** where you can hang your hats and coats. On your right is the living room, and this door on your left leads into a small dining room. As you can see, it has a lovely wooden **floor**. The dining room and the kitchen are connected, so you can cook in the kitchen and serve the meals in the dining room. From the kitchen **window** you have a nice view of the **backyard**, which, as you can see, has a wooden **fence** around it. You could have a nice flower or vegetable **garden** back there.

"The house is in excellent condition. You'll have no problems with any of the **walls**, floors or **ceilings**. So, any questions? Ah, yes, the price. Three bedrooms, a garage and a yard. Well, what do you think?

Exercise 1

Label the parts of the house with the letters from the list on the left.

a) the kitchen
b) the backyard
c) the driveway
d) the living room
e) the front yard
f) the garage
g) the dining room
h) the stairs
i) the front door
j) the walk

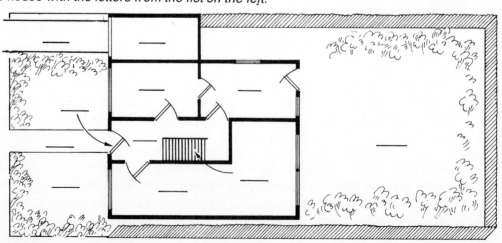

Exercise 2

What are these rooms used for? Match each part of the house with what usually happens in it.

1 _____ the kitchen		a)	a place to wash
2 _____ the dining room		b)	a place to sleep
3 _____ the bedroom		c)	a place to hang coats
4 _____ the garage		d)	a place to relax and talk
5 _____ the garden		e)	a place to cook
6 _____ the bathroom		f)	a place to grow flowers
7 _____ the living room		g)	a place to keep a car
8 _____ the hall		h)	a place to eat

Exercise 3

Which part of the house is different from the other three in each group?

1	a) floor	b) wall	c) stairs	d) ceiling
2	a) fireplace	b) roof	c) furnace	d) chimney
3	a) bathroom	b) garage	c) kitchen	d) bedroom
4	a) window	b) wall	c) gate	d) door
5	a) downstairs	b) upstairs	c) basement	d) story
6	a) fence	b) driveway	c) hedge	d) wall

Just for fun

Which would you most like to have in a house? Put the following in order from most important (1) to least important (6). Then discuss your answers with someone else.

a large bedroom _____   a large comfortable living room _____

a large modern kitchen _____   a large bathroom   _____

a large backyard _____   a garage   _____

Think about

1 Think of a house you know and describe it to a classmate. Then ask your classmate to draw a plan of the house.

2 How much does the average house cost in your country? What makes one house more expensive than another?

3 Describe a very traditional type of house in your country.

1.2 Furniture and furnishings

Words in context *Read the following dialogue and do the exercises.*

It is the twenty-fifth century. A group of children is visiting the National Museum of the Past.
One child has a lot of questions for the tour guide.

GUIDE: We are now entering a typical living room of the late twentieth century.

CHILD: What's that box in the middle of the room? And why are all those **chairs** in front of it?

GUIDE: That box is called a **television**. People used to look at the pictures on it for hours and hours. They used to sit in those **arm-chairs** or on the **sofa**, which is that big chair for two or three people.

CHILD: Did people have machines for listening to music in those days, like we do now?

GUIDE: Yes, of course. This machine in the corner is called a **stereo**. It has four parts. This part on top was used for playing round black disks called **records**. Underneath that, you can see the **radio**. Underneath the radio, there's a **cassette player**, which was used for playing music on tape. And underneath the cassette player, there's a **compact disc player**. It was used for playing music recorded on small round disks called **CD**'s.

CHILD: What's that low **table** in front of the sofa? Is that a kind of **desk**?

GUIDE: No, their desks were much bigger, and they had **drawers**. That's called a **coffee table**. In those days people used to drink something called coffee and smoke things called cigarettes. They used to put their cof-fee cups on this table while they were watching television. They dropped the ash from their cigarettes into that glass dish. That's why it's called an **ashtray**. Coffee and cigarettes have been illegal for the last two hundred and fifty years.

CHILD: And what are those things on the **shelves** over there behind the **dining table**? Are they books?

GUIDE: Yes, they are. And the piece of furniture with the shelves is called a **bookcase**.

CHILD: Didn't they have **computers**?

GUIDE: Yes, they did. Personal computers were in-vented towards the end of the century and revolutionized everyone's lives. Now then, I'd like someone to turn off that old **lamp** by pushing the **switch** on its side. I'll close the **curtains** to make the room a bit darker and we'll turn on this television and watch a very popular twentieth-century movie for children. It's about a mouse called Mickey.

Exercise 1

Circle those things which probably do not exist in the twenty-fifth century, according to the conversation between the guide and the child.

1 books

2 coffee

3 televisions

4 chairs

5 desks

6 curtains

7 records

8 radios

9 computers

10 sofas

11 shelves

12 machines for playing music

13 cigarettes

14 dining tables

15 Mickey Mouse movies

Exercise 2

Match the words with the pictures.

| a) armchair | b) dining table | c) lamp | d) switch | e) bookcase | f) desk | g) sofa | h) drawer |

1 _____ 2 _____ 3 _____ 4 _____

5 _____ 6 _____ 7 _____ 8 _____

Exercise 3

Complete the sentences using the words below.

| ashtray | compact disc player | stereo | cassette player | coffee table | shelf |

1 Put the book on the _____.

2 Put the record on the _____.

3 Put the cup on the _____.

4 Put out your cigarette in the _____.

5 Put the tape in the _____.

6 Put the CD in the _____.

Dictionary work

Put the following items into the correct columns. Do as many as you can and then check your answers in a dictionary.

| a deckchair | a closet | a wardrobe | a stool | a carpet | a cabinet |
| a bench | a chest of drawers | a rug | a mat | a cushion | linoleum |

to sit on	to put things in	to walk on
_____	_____	_____
_____	_____	_____
_____	_____	_____
_____	_____	_____

Think about

1 What furniture do you have in your living room?

2 What furniture do you usually find in the different rooms of a house in your country?

3 Do you have a television, a stereo, a telephone? If you could have only one of these things, which would you choose?

1.3 Sleeping

Words in context *Read the following passage and do the exercises.*

It's late. You're **tired**. It's been a long day and you're ready to **go to bed**. You're feeling **sleepy**. You can hardly keep your eyes open. So you take your clothes off, put on your **pajamas**, brush your teeth, wash your hands and face, and get ready to get into bed. You pull back the **blankets**, get in between the **sheets** and rest your head on the **pillow**.

The **mattress** under you feels just right, not too hard and not too soft. Maybe you start reading a book, but you're **exhausted**, and in a few minutes your eyes get heavy. You can't stay **awake** any longer. You start to get **drowsy**. You turn the light out and soon, very soon, you begin to **fall asleep**. You are half asleep already. And then quite suddenly you move from **consciousness** to **unconsciousness** and you are asleep.

(Now answer question I, Exercise I.)

But then what happens?

In the first hour of a normal night's sleep, you go into a **deep sleep**. In fact, this is the time when your sleep is deepest. Then, later in the night, the mind goes into a lighter sleep, called by scientists ''paradoxical sleep.'' It is during this type of sleep that you have your **dreams** (or **nightmares**!). In a normal night, most people go from deep sleep to paradoxical sleep about four or five times. Each period of deep sleep becomes less deep and shorter, and each period of paradoxical sleep becomes longer and lighter. Finally you have your last period of paradoxical sleep and your last dream. Then you **wake up**. And now that you are awake, it's time to **get up**.

(Now answer question 2.)

Exercise 1

1 *Name the things in the pictures.*

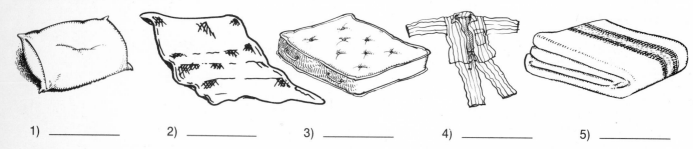

1) _____ 2) _____ 3) _____ 4) _____ 5) _____

2 *Look at these diagrams. Which one shows a normal night's sleep?*

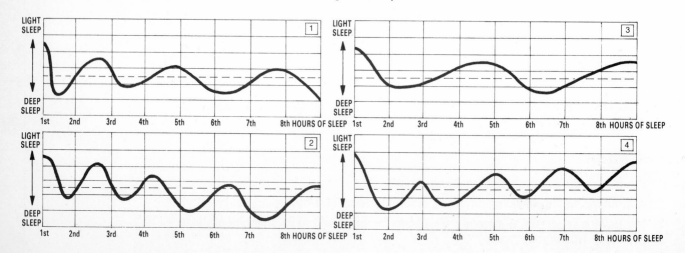

Exercise 2

Match each word or phrase on the left with a word or phrase of similar meaning on the right.

1 _____ in a conscious state	a) get out of bed
2 _____ bad dream	b) lie down
3 _____ go to bed	c) sleepy
4 _____ drowsy	d) awake
5 _____ in an unconscious state	e) exhausted
6 _____ get up	f) nightmare
7 _____ very tired	g) asleep

Exercise 3

Put these events in the most likely order.

1 First, you _____	a) have a dream.
2 Then, you _____	b) go into a deep sleep.
3 So, you _____	c) wake up.
4 After a while, you _____	d) fall asleep.
5 Later, you might _____	e) are tired.
6 Finally, you begin to _____	f) feel sleepy.

Just for fun

Look at this list and decide whether these are good or bad things to do before going to sleep.

	very bad --------- very good				
1 eat a meal	1	2	3	4	5
2 read a book	1	2	3	4	5
3 take a sleeping pill	1	2	3	4	5
4 drink a cup of coffee	1	2	3	4	5
5 do some physical exercises	1	2	3	4	5
6 do your homework	1	2	3	4	5
7 drink a cup of hot milk	1	2	3	4	5

Discuss your answers with someone else. Can you think of other things that help you sleep well, or that keep you from falling asleep?

Think about

1 What time do you usually go to bed? Do you fall asleep easily? Do you usually sleep well?

2 Do you usually remember your dreams? Have you had any strange dreams or nightmares that you can remember? Why do you think we dream?

1.4 Washing

Words in context *Read the following passage and do the exercises.*

These days many people start their day by going into the bathroom to **wash**. They turn on a **faucet** and hot water runs into the **sink**. They pick up a **bar of soap** and wash their hands and face. They take a **towel** to **dry themselves**. Then they put **toothpaste** on their **toothbrush** in order to **brush their teeth**. Not so long ago, however, many homes did not have bathrooms at all. Soap was something that only rich families could afford, and people did not think it was necessary to brush their teeth.

Today we think it is important to be clean, but there was a long period of history when almost no one **took a bath** or a **shower**. Queen Isabella of Spain (1451–1504) took only two baths in her life, one on the day she was born and the other on the day she was married. Queen Elizabeth I of England (1533–1603) is said to have taken only one bath in her whole life. There was no bathtub in the White House until 1831 and no bathroom in Buckingham Palace until after 1837. There were even some religious groups who thought that taking a bath was a crime against God.

However, wearing **perfume** to smell nice has always been popular, ever since the time of the ancient Egyptian five thousand years ago. Of course, if you think about how often people washed, you will realize why perfume was so necessary.

Exercise 1

Choose the word or phrase in parentheses which will make each sentence true according to the information in the passage. Circle the word or phrase as in the example.

Example: (Nowadays/~~In the past~~) most homes (~~don't~~/didn't) have hot water.

1 (Nowadays/In the past) most homes (have/had) bathrooms.

2 (Nowadays/In the past) most people never (brush/brushed) their teeth.

3 (Nowadays/In the past) most people (wash/washed) every day.

4 (Nowadays/In the past) most people (don't/didn't) use soap.

5 (Nowadays/In the past) most kings and queens of Europe (don't/didn't) take baths.

6 (Nowadays/In the past) most people (believe/believed) that it (is/was) important to be clean.

7 (Nowadays/In the past) most people (need/needed) to wear perfume.

Exercise 2

Look at the pictures. Write what each thing is and what it is used for.

	thing	used for
1	_____	_____ your _____
2	_____	_____ yourself
3	_____	_____ yourself
4	_____	_____ a _____

Exercise 3

Match the things on the left with the descriptions on the right.

1 _____	toothpaste	a)	You wash your hands in it.
2 _____	sink	b)	Water comes out of it when you turn it on.
3 _____	perfume	c)	You clean your teeth with it.
4 _____	shower	d)	It smells nice.
5 _____	bathtub	e)	You stand under it.
6 _____	faucet	f)	You sit in it.

Dictionary work

The things on the left are used on the different parts of the body on the right. Match each item with a part of the body. More than one answer may be possible, but there is always one best answer. Do as many as you can and then check your answers in a dictionary.

1 _____	lipstick	a)	on a man's face before shaving
2 _____	shaving cream	b)	under the arms
3 _____	shampoo	c)	on the fingernails
4 _____	nail polish	d)	on the hair
5 _____	deodorant	e)	on a man's shaved chin and cheeks
6 _____	aftershave	f)	on the eyes and cheeks
7 _____	make-up	g)	on the mouth

Think about

1 Do you prefer to take a shower or a bath?

2 What do you do to get ready to go out in the morning? How long do you take to get ready?

3 Do you use make-up and perfume? When, why and what kind?

1.5 Housework

Words in context *Read the following passage and do the exercises.*

Mr. and Mrs. Turvey both hated housework. They were a very **messy** couple who never put things away. When they went to bed, for example, they always left their clothes on the floor. Their kitchen was always a mess, too. Even though they had a **dishwasher**, they always left the **dirty** dishes in the kitchen sink and only **did the dishes** when there wasn't a **clean** plate in the house. It was the same with their clothes. They never put them into the **washing machine** until there was nothing else left to wear. The living room always looked as though a bomb had just gone off. There were things everywhere. There was thick **dust** on every piece of furniture and the carpet had not been **vacuumed** for weeks.

And the bathroom!

One day, when Mr. Turvey couldn't find one of his shoes, and Mrs. Turvey couldn't see her face in the bathroom mirror, they decided it was time to get the house **cleaned**. So they found Maria, a foreign student at a local language school, who needed some extra money.

Maria came to the house and worked all day long. She washed and dried all the clothes. Then she got out the **iron**. She **ironed** the clothes, folded them neatly and put them away. She **swept** all the dust off the floors with a large **broom**. She took a wet **cloth** and **wiped** the dust off every surface in the house and then **polished** the furniture until it was **shining**. She got out the **vacuum cleaner** and vacuumed all the carpets. In the kitchen the floor was **filthy**. It was too dirty to wash with a **mop**, so Maria got on her hands and knees and **scrubbed** the dirt off with a **scrub brush**. Finally, she **made the bed** and, when she finished, the house looked **spotless**.

Mr. and Mrs. Turvey came home that evening. There was nothing on the floor. There was no dust on the furniture. The wood was shining and you could smell the **polish**. In their bedroom all their clothes were clean and put away in closets. "So what do you think?" Mrs. Turvey asked her husband.

"It looks nice and **neat**," he said, "but how are we ever going to find anything?"

Exercise 1

Put these pictures into the order in which they are described in the story.

1 _____   2 _____   3 _____   4 _____   5 _____   6 _____   7 _____

Exercise 2

Put these words and phrases into the sentences. You may use the same word more than once.

spotless	dirty	neat	filthy	messy	clean

1 _____ is almost opposite in meaning to _____

2 _____ is almost opposite in meaning to _____

3 _____ is almost opposite in meaning to _____

4 _____ means very, very _____

5 _____ means very, very _____

Exercise 3

What do you use to clean the house? Match the objects in the box with the actions below. More than one answer may be possible, but there is always one best answer.

a) a broom	c) a vacuum cleaner	e) polish	g) a mop	i) a scrub brush
b) a dishwasher	d) a washing machine	f) a cloth	h) an iron	

1 _____ to wash clothes

2 _____ to sweep the floor

3 _____ to make clothes smooth

4 _____ to scrub the floor

5 _____ to do the dishes

6 _____ to wash the kitchen floor

7 _____ to clean the carpet

8 _____ to wipe surfaces

9 _____ to make furniture shiny

Just for fun

Imagine you are working for a company that makes products used in housework. It is your job to think of a name and an advertising description for new products.

> *Example:* a new type of vacuum cleaner.
> Name: Vroom
> Sentence: Vroom gets your dirty carpet clean in seconds.

Think of names and write sentences for these products.

1 a laundry detergent
2 a furniture polish

3 a dish washing liquid
4 a dishwasher

5 an iron

Think about

1 Are you a neat person?

2 Who does most of the housework in your home? What kind of housework do you do and how often?

3 What kind of housework do you most hate doing? What kind of housework do you least mind doing?

4 Which of the following machines is the most useful for housework: a dishwasher, a washing machine, a vacuum cleaner?

Vocabulary review

1 At home (Units 1.1–1.5)

1.1 Parts of the house
backyard
basement
bathroom
bedroom
ceiling
chimney
dining room
downstairs
driveway
fence
fireplace
floor
front door
front yard
furnace
garage
garden
gate
hall
hedge
kitchen
living room
roof
story
upstairs
walk *n*
wall
window

1.2 Furniture and furnishings
armchair
ashtray
bench
bookcase
cabinet
carpet
cassette player
CD
chair
chest of drawers
closet
coffee table
compact disc player
computer
curtain
cushion
deckchair
desk
dining table
drawer
lamp
linoleum
mat
radio
record
rug
shelf
sofa
stereo
stool
switch
table
television
wardrobe

1.3 Sleeping
asleep
awake
bed
    go to bed
blanket
consciousness
deep sleep
dream
drowsy
exhausted
fall asleep
get up
mattress
nightmare
pajamas
pillow
sheet
sleepy
tired
unconsciousness
wake up

1.4 Washing
aftershave
bar of soap
bath
    take a bath
bathtub
brush your teeth
deodorant
dry yourself
faucet
lipstick
make-up
nail polish
perfume
shampoo
shaving cream
shower
    take a shower
sink
toothbrush
toothpaste
towel
wash

1.5 Housework
bed
    make the bed
broom
clean
cloth
dirty
dishes
    do the dishes
dishwater
dust
filthy
iron
mess
messy
mop
neat
polish
scrub
scrub brush
shine
spotless
sweep
vacuum
vacuum cleaner
washing machine
wipe

Test yourself 1

Use the words from the **Vocabulary review** to help you fill in the blanks in these sentences. The number of dashes corresponds to the number of letters in the missing word. More than one answer may be possible, but there is always one best answer.

1 Grandfather sat in his favorite _ _ _ _ _ _ _ _ in front of the open fire.

2 I'm afraid you can't put your car in my _ _ _ _ _ _. It's full.

3 The rain is coming through the _ _ _ _ _ _ _ in the upstairs bedroom.

4 My aunt's kitchen floor is always _ _ _ _ _ _ _ _. It's so clean you could eat a meal off it.

5 I like the taste of this new _ _ _ _ _ _ _ _ _ _. I'm going to brush my teeth with it every morning from now on.

6 He decided to _ _ _ _ _ _ every piece of furniture in the house.

7 If you put a _ _ _ _ _ _ _ on that chair, I think you'll find it much more comfortable.

8 It may get very cold tonight, so take another _ _ _ _ _ _ _ for your bed.

9 Do you like the smell of her _ _ _ _ _ _ _? She always puts it on before she goes out.

10 They played football on a wet, muddy field and came home with _ _ _ _ _ _ clothes.

11 If you leave your umbrella in the _ _ _ _, you'll remember it when you leave the house.

12 Do you prefer to sleep on a hard or a soft _ _ _ _ _ _ _ _?

13 She's not very _ _ _ _. She always leaves her room in a mess.

14 Are you going to take a shower? Here's a clean _ _ _ _ _ _.

15 That shirt is too wrinkled to wear. Why don't you _ _ _ _ it?

16 Last night I had a terrible _ _ _ _ _ _ _ _ _. I dreamed a monster was chasing me.

17 It's very dark in here. Why don't you open the _ _ _ _ _ _ _ _ and let in some light.

18 My grandmother never had a _ _ _ _ _ _ _ _ _ _ or a washing machine. She washed all the dishes and the clothes by hand in the kitchen sink.

19 We need to buy some more _ _ _ _ immediately. There isn't any left in the bathroom and I want to take a bath.

20 If you put the television antenna on the _ _ _ _ you'll get a much better picture.

21 After running ten miles, she was absolutely _ _ _ _ _ _ _ _ _.

22 I'm feeling very _ _ _ _ _ _. I think I'll go to bed.

23 You'll find the light _ _ _ _ _ _ by the side of the bed. Turn it on, would you?

24 It took the actor two hours to put on his _ _ _ _ _-_ _.

25 You'll find a pencil and some paper in my _ _ _ _.

1.6 Cooking

Words in context *Read the following passage and do the exercises.*

Here are five simple ways to cook an EGG

❊❊❊ BOILED EGGS ❊❊❊

One of the easiest things to make is a boiled egg. Put an egg into a **saucepan** full of cold water. Put the saucepan on top of the **stove**. Turn on the heat. When the water starts to **boil**, look at your watch. You should boil the water fast for about three to four minutes only. Then remove the egg immediately from the water and serve.

❊❊❊ EGG SALAD ❊❊❊

To make egg salad, boil an egg in water for about eight to ten minutes. When the egg is cold, **peel** off the egg shell and cut up the egg. **Chop** a little piece of onion with a sharp **knife**.

Then **mix** the egg and onion with some mayonnaise. Now you have egg salad. Put this on some fresh bread with some - thinly **sliced** tomato and you have a great sandwich.

❊❊❊ FRIED EGGS ❊❊❊

Melt a little butter or oil in a **frying pan**. Break the egg into the pan, without breaking its yellow center. **Fry** it quickly. This is a very popular breakfast dish in the United States and Great Britain, where it is often served with toast and bacon.

❊❊❊ SCRAMBLED EGGS ❊❊❊

Scrambled eggs are also popular. First, **beat** two eggs together with a little milk. Melt some butter in a frying pan and **pour** in the mixture. **Stir** with a wooden **spoon** and cook until the egg starts to get thick. Make sure you have some buttered toast ready to eat with your eggs.

❊❊❊ BAKED EGGS ❊❊❊

Eggs can also be **baked** in the **oven**. **Heat** the oven first. Break the egg and pour it into a special oven dish. Add a small spoonful of melted butter or cream, or **grate** some cheese over it, and bake it in the oven for eight or ten minutes.

Exercise 1

Match each picture with one of the ways of cooking an egg described in the passage.

1 _____

2 _____

3 _____

4 _____

5 _____

Exercise 2

Use these words to complete the sentences. You may use each word more than once.

| knife | oven | spoon | saucepan | frying pan | stove |

1 You can bake food in the _____.

2 You can slice food with a _____.

3 You can fry food in a _____.

4 You can heat food on top of the _____.

5 You can mix food with a _____.

6 You can boil water in a _____.

7 You can chop food with a _____.

8 You can stir food with a _____.

9 You can peel food with a _____.

Exercise 3

Which verbs can be used with these foods?
Match the foods on the left with the actions on the right.

1 milk _____ _____

2 bread _____

3 an orange _____ _____

4 butter _____

5 soup _____ _____

6 a tomato _____ _____ _____

7 cheese _____ _____ _____

8 an onion _____ _____ _____ _____

a) slice

b) grate

c) chop

d) pour

e) melt

f) stir

g) peel

Dictionary work

Decide whether each of these foods is a type of fruit (F), vegetable (V), or meat (M). Do as many as you can and then check your answers in a dictionary.

_____ sausage _____ ham _____ grape _____ pea _____ bean

_____ pineapple _____ celery _____ lamb _____ cabbage _____ beef

_____ strawberry _____ steak _____ peach _____ spinach _____ avocado

_____ turkey _____ veal _____ pear _____ cucumber _____ plum

Think about

1 Can you cook? Do you enjoy cooking? Why? Why not?

2 What's your favorite food?

3 Which food do you know how to cook best? How do you prepare it?

4 Describe something that people eat every day in your country. How is it prepared?

1.7 Eating

Words in context

Read the following passage and do the exercises.

Before John and Susie Barker went to visit their grandmother, their mother told them that their grandmother thought children should have good table manners. So she wrote out this list of instructions.

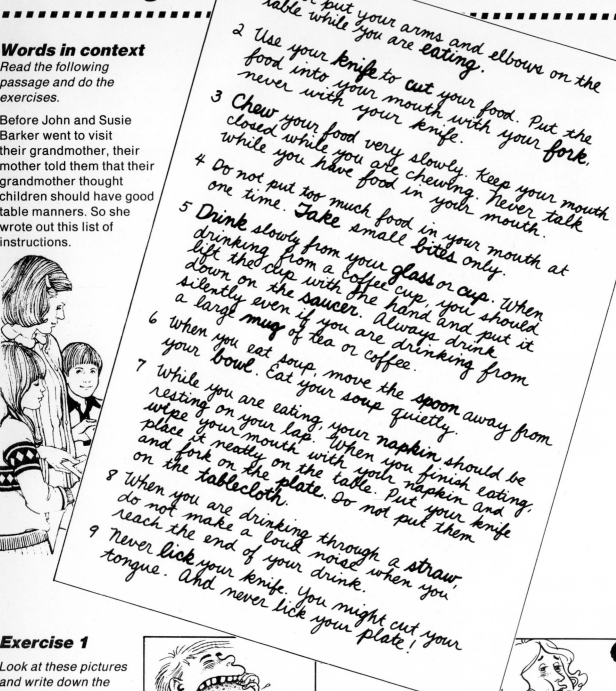

1 Do not put your arms and elbows on the table while you are **eating**.

2 Use your **knife** to **cut** your food. Put the food into your mouth with your **fork**, never with your knife.

3 **Chew** your food very slowly. Keep your mouth closed while you are chewing. Never talk while you have food in your mouth.

4 Do not put too much food in your mouth at one time. **Take** small **bites** only.

5 **Drink** slowly from your **glass** or **cup**. When drinking from a coffee cup, you should lift the cup with one hand and put it down on the **saucer**. Always drink silently even if you are drinking from a large **mug** of tea or coffee.

6 When you eat soup, move the **spoon** away from your **bowl**. Eat your soup quietly.

7 While you are eating, your **napkin** should be resting on your lap. When you finish eating, wipe your mouth with your napkin and place it neatly on the table. Put your knife and fork on the **plate**. Do not put them on the **tablecloth**.

8 When you are drinking through a **straw**, do not make a loud noise when you reach the end of your drink.

9 Never **lick** your knife. You might cut your tongue. And never lick your plate!

Exercise 1

Look at these pictures and write down the number of the rule that has been broken.

a) _____

b) _____

c) _____

d) _____

e) _____

Exercise 2

Match each action on the left with the right noun on the right.

1 You take a bite with _____

2 You lick with _____

3 You eat soup with a _____

4 You cover your lap with _____

5 You cover the table with _____

6 You place a cup on _____

7 You drink through _____

8 You cut your food with _____

9 You put your knife and fork together on _____

10 You drink hot chocolate out of _____

11 You put your breakfast cereal in _____

12 You chew with _____

a) a spoon.

b) a saucer.

c) a mug.

d) your plate.

e) your front teeth.

f) your back teeth.

g) a bowl.

h) a napkin.

i) a knife.

j) a tablecloth.

k) your tongue.

l) a straw.

Just for fun

Look at this list and decide whether these are good or bad eating habits. Discuss your answers with someone else.

	very good ---------- very bad				
1 eating while you are standing up	1	2	3	4	5
2 a vegetarian diet of fruit and vegetables	1	2	3	4	5
3 eating fried foods	1	2	3	4	5
4 having a large lunch every day	1	2	3	4	5
5 putting salt on your food	1	2	3	4	5
6 drinking three cups of strong coffee every day	1	2	3	4	5
7 drinking fresh orange juice every day	1	2	3	4	5
8 drinking one glass of wine every day	1	2	3	4	5
9 eating very slowly, chewing many times	1	2	3	4	5
10 eating when you are nervous or worried	1	2	3	4	5
11 having no breakfast in the morning	1	2	3	4	5

Think about

1 Compare the table manners and eating habits in your country with those in some other countries that you have visited or heard about.

2 When are the different meal times in your country? What is usually served?

3 Can you describe a healthy diet?

1.8 Keeping food fresh

Words in context *Read the following passage and do the exercises.*

Food which is left open to the air will **go bad** unless something is done to keep it **fresh**. Some foods go bad very quickly. Milk and other milk products will **turn sour** in a few hours. **Raw** meat will go bad in about a day. Bread, cake and other similar foods will **go stale** in a couple of days. Even many fruits and vegetables start to **rot** in less than a week. It has always been important, therefore, to find ways of preserving food in order to keep it fresh and **delicious**.

Some methods of preserving food are very old. For example, food was **dried, smoked** or **salted** thousands of years ago. But it was in the early nineteenth century that many of the methods that we use today were invented.

In 1810, a Frenchman, Nicholas Appert, discovered a way of keeping food fresh by putting it in **bottles** and glass **jars**. The **bottled** food was heated and no air was allowed to get in. In 1834, Peter Durand, an Englishman, invented the process of **canning**. He managed to preserve food in air-free metal **cans**. Finally, in 1851, an American called John Gorrie invented the refrigerator, so that food could be kept cold or **frozen**. Together, these three men and their inventions (bottled, **canned**, and frozen food) have had an enormous effect on what we eat and the way food is bought and sold today.

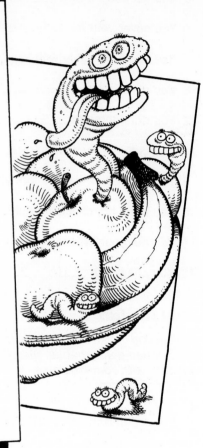

Exercise 1

Complete the paragraph with words taken from the passage. Use only one word in each blank space.

There are many different ways of preventing food from going (1)_____. Some of them are

(2)_____ of years old. Several important methods were invented in the (3)_____

century. First, a Frenchman discovered a way to keep food (4)_____ in glass (5)_____.

A few years later an Englishman invented canning, in which food is preserved in air-free (6)_____

cans. Finally, John Gorrie invented the (7)_____. In the refrigerator, milk will take much

longer to turn (8)_____ and meat will take several days to (9)_____. And

(10)_____ food, which has been kept in the freezer, may not go bad for years.

Exercise 2

The adjectives "bad" or "not fresh" can be used to describe most types of food. Some other adjectives are usually used only with particular types of food. Put each word below in one of the three columns. Looking back at the passage will help you.

| tomatoes | cream | ham | cake | cookies | chicken | milk | bananas |

        sour   **stale**   **rotten**

1 _____ 3 _____ 5 _____ 7 _____

2 _____ 4 _____ 6 _____ 8 _____

Exercise 3

Match each word in the box with its definition below.

| a) raw | b) dried | c) delicious | d) smoked | e) frozen | f) canned | g) salted | h) bottled |

1 _____ kept in air-free metal containers

2 _____ kept below 32°F

3 _____ uncooked

4 _____ tasting good

5 _____ kept in air-free glass containers

6 _____ containing no water or liquid

7 _____ heated over a wood fire

8 _____ kept in salt

Dictionary work

Match the containers with the pictures. To help you, the typical contents of each container have also been given. Do as many as you can and then check your answers in a dictionary.

a) a jar (of honey)
b) a bottle (of ketchup)
c) a box (of chocolate)

d) a can (of peas)
e) a mug (of hot coffee)
f) a glass (of cold water)

g) a package (of crackers)
h) a cup (of tea)
i) a kettle (of hot water)

j) a bowl (of cooked rice)
k) a carton (of milk)
l) a bag (of apples)

1 ____ 3 ____ 5 ____ 7 ____ 9 ____ 11 ____

2 ____ 4 ____ 6 ____ 8 ____ 10 ____ 12 ____

Think about

1 How many different ways of preserving food can you describe?

2 Are there any ways of preserving food that you think are bad for you? What are they?

3 How and where do you keep the following foods in your home: cheese, milk, bread, tea, coffee, fruit, fresh green vegetables, fresh fruit?

1.9 Clothes

Words in context   *Read the following passages and do the exercises.*

Not so long ago, in many countries, children went to school wearing a school uniform. Boys wore a white **shirt** and a **tie**, a dark **jacket**, gray **pants** and black **shoes**. Girls used to wear a white **blouse** and a dark, knee-length **skirt**. Today, in many countries, students have a very different kind of uniform. They wear **tennis shoes**, **jeans**, and a **T-shirt**. On a hot day students might even come to class in a pair of **shorts**. Teachers in the past would never have allowed these students into their class. Then, the men teachers used to wear a **suit** and tie, and most women teachers wore a **dress** or skirt. But when you look inside a classroom today, it is sometimes difficult to tell who are the teachers and who are the students!

(Now answer questions 1, 2 and 3 in Exercise 1.)

People from hot sunny countries often find it difficult to imagine how people who live in a very cold climate can live and work through the winter months. These people manage because they know what to wear in the cold. First, it is very important to keep your head, hands and feet warm. So everyone has a **hat,** thick **gloves** to keep their hands warm, and a pair of long **socks** and heavy **boots** for their feet. Of course, you should have a heavy **overcoat** and you should wear a thick wool **sweater** under it. A **scarf** around the neck also helps to keep out the cold. What you wear under your clothes is important, too. People who live in cold climates always wear long **underwear**. Long underwear may not be very comfortable, but it certainly keeps your legs warm!

(Now answer questions 4, 5 and 6.)

Exercise 1

Decide whether the following statements are true (T) or false (F) according to the information in the passages.

1 _____ In the past, many female students wore white blouses to school.

2 _____ Today, teachers never allow students to wear jeans to class.

3 _____ Today, many teachers wear the same kind of clothes to school as their students.

4 _____ In many cold countries people wear long socks over their hands and gloves over their feet.

5 _____ In cold weather it's a good idea to wear shorts.

6 _____ In cold weather it's a good idea to wear a scarf.

Exercise 2

Name the articles of clothing in the pictures.

1 _____ 2 _____ 3 _____ 4 _____ 5 _____ 6 _____

Exercise 3

In chart 1, decide whether the clothes are usually worn above the waist, below the waist, or both above and below the waist. In chart 2, decide whether the clothes are usually worn by women or by both men and women. Use X's to fill in the charts.

Chart 1

		above waist	below waist	above and below
1	jeans			
2	suit			
3	dress			
4	tie			
5	shorts			
6	scarf			
7	skirt			
8	underwear			
9	shirt			

Chart 2

		women only	both men and women
1	T-shirt		
2	underwear		
3	jeans		
4	blouse		
5	dress		
6	boots		
7	jacket		
8	gloves		
9	skirt		

Just for fun

Which item of clothing is different from the other three in each group? More than one answer may be possible. Discuss your answers with someone else.

1 a) shoes   b) socks   c) gloves   d) shirt
2 a) socks   b) jeans   c) pants   d) shorts
3 a) underwear   b) blouse   c) sweater   d) dress
4 a) scarf   b) hat   c) overcoat   d) tie
5 a) tie   b) dress   c) suit   d) T-shirt

Think about

1 How does a typical businessman/woman dress in your country?
2 What do children usually wear to school in your country?
3 What clothes do you wear when it is a) very cold b) very wet c) very hot?
4 Describe the traditional clothes or national costume of your country.

1.10 Fashions

Words in context *Read the following passage and do the exercises.*

Spring, summer, autumn, winter: every season there are new clothes and new fashions in the stores. Colors and styles keep changing. One season black is the "**in**" color, but the next season everyone is wearing orange or pink or gray. One season **tight-fitting** clothes are **fashionable**, and the next season **baggy** clothes are "in."

The length of women's skirts goes up and down from year to year. In the 1960s, mini-skirts became very fashionable and a woman could wear a skirt eight or nine inches above the knee. A few years later, maxi-skirts became **popular** and then you had to wear skirts eight or nine inches below the knee. Each season there is always a "correct" length and if your skirt is just a little too long or too short some people will think that you are very **unfashionable**.

Men have similar problems with their shirts. Some years it is fashionable to wear very small collars. Another year small collars become **out-dated** and large **button-down** collars are popular. Sometimes it even becomes fashionable to wear shirts with no collars at all. A shirt that you once thought was very **modern** can look strangely **old-fashioned** a few years later. And your father's shirts, which you always thought were very **conservative** and **traditional**, can suddenly seem very **stylish**.

Keeping up with the fashions can be very expensive. So one way to save money is never to throw your old clothes out. If you wait long enough, the clothes that are **out of style** today will be back **in style** tomorrow. Yesterday's clothes are tomorrow's new fashions.

Exercise 1

Choose the best answer according to the information in the passage.

1 New fashions come out every
   a) year   b) season   c) two years

2 Tight-fitting clothes are
   a) always in fashion   b) sometimes unfashionable
   c) always conservative

3 The fashionable length for a woman's skirt depends on
   a) the year   b) the woman's height
   c) the color of the skirt

4 You can tell if a man's shirt is in style by looking at
   a) the collar   b) the buttons   c) the color

5 It's a good idea to keep your parents' old clothes because
   a) they are conservative
   b) the style might be "in" again in a few year's time
   c) it is always fashionable to wear old-fashioned clothes

Exercise 2

Put these words and phrases into two columns depending on whether they can be used to describe a modern or an old style.

in style	old-fashioned	conservative	out of style
stylish	popular	outdated	in

modern   **old**

_____   _____

_____   _____

_____   _____

_____   _____

Exercise 3

Complete the following sentences as in the example.

Example: A _friendly_ person likes to make friends.

1 A(n) _____ person likes to follow traditions.

2 A(n) _____ person doesn't like to follow traditions.

3 A(n) _____ person likes to wear new styles.

4 A(n) _____ shirt is soft and shapeless like a bag.

Dictionary work

Match the styles with the pictures. Do as many as you can and then check your answers in a dictionary.

a) short-sleeved	d) checked	g) striped	j) turtle neck
b) high-heeled	e) button-down	h) V-neck	k) pleated
c) belted	f) baggy	i) tight-fitting	l) flowered

1 _____   2 _____   3 _____   4 _____   5 _____   6 _____

 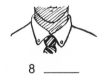  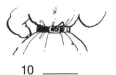 

7 _____   8 _____   9 _____   10 _____   11 _____   12 _____

Think about

1 Do you like shopping for clothes? Why? Why not?

2 What clothes are you and your friends wearing at the moment?

3 What styles and colors are fashionable at the moment for men and for women?

4 What was in style last year, but is out of style this year?

Vocabulary review

1 At home (Units 1.6–1.10)

1.6 Cooking

avocado
bake
bean
beat
beef
boil
cabbage
celery
cucumber
fry
frying pan
grape
grate
ham
heat
knife
lamb
melt
mix
oven
pea
peach
pear
peel
pineapple
plum
pour
saucepan
sausage
slice
spinach
spoon
steak
stir
stove
strawberry
turkey
veal

1.7 Eating

bite
bowl
chew
coffee cup
cup
cut
drink
eat
fork
glass

knife
lick
mug
napkin
plate
saucer
spoon
straw
tablecloth

1.8 Keeping food fresh

bad
  go bad
bag
bottle
bowl
box
can
canned
canning
carton
cup
delicious
dried
fresh
frozen
glass
jar
kettle
mug
package
raw
rot
rotten
salted
smoked
sour
  turn sour
stale
  go stale

1.9 Clothes

blouse
boot
dress
glove
hat
jacket
jeans
overcoat
pants
scarf
shirt
shoe
shorts
skirt
sock
suit
sweater
tennis shoe
tie
T-shirt
underwear

1.10 Fashions

baggy
belted
button-down
checked
conservative
fashionable
flowered
high-heeled
in *adj*
in style
modern
old-fashioned
out-dated
out of style
pleated
popular
short-sleeved
striped
stylish
tight-fitting
traditional
turtle neck
unfashionable
V-neck

Test yourself 2

Use the words from the **Vocabulary review** to help you fill in the blanks in these sentences. The number of dashes corresponds to the number of letters in the missing word. More than one answer may be possible, but there is always one best answer.

1 He likes to follow fashion and always wears _ _ _ _ _ _ _ clothes.

2 When you heat water to 212°F it _ _ _ _ _.

3 My parents always told me to _ _ _ _ my food thirty-two times before swallowing it.

4 It's very hot in here. Do you mind if I take off my jacket and _ _ _?

5 He has some very _ _ _-_ _ _ _ _ _ _ _ _ ideas about what people should and should not wear.

6 Have you ever eaten _ _ _ fish? It's very popular in Japan.

7 Instant coffee is very easy to make. Simply put the coffee into a cup and _ _ _ _ in the hot water.

8 The friendly dog went up to the little girl and started to _ _ _ _ her face.

9 At the moment women are wearing very short skirts, but they probably won't be in _ _ _ _ _ for very long.

10 This bread is incredibly _ _ _ _ _ _. I almost broke my teeth on it.

11 Do businessmen in your country always wear a _ _ _ _ _ to work?

12 I don't eat _ _ _ because in my religion we are not allowed to eat the meat of the pig.

13 In the late 1960s it was very _ _ _ _ _ _ _ _ _ _ _ _ for men to have long hair.

14 Let's put her Christmas present in this white, cardboard _ _ _.

15 Which _ _ _ _ _ _ _ should I put on the table for our guests tonight — the paper ones or the cloth ones?

16 It's very cold outside. Why don't you wear a _ _ _?

17 The water in the lake is _ _ _ _ _ _ because it was so cold last night.

18 The sun is out now and the snow has started to _ _ _ _ _.

19 This milk doesn't smell very good. I think it turned _ _ _ _.

20 The honey in that glass _ _ _ is made by the bees in this area.

21 She wore a long, black evening _ _ _ _ _ _ to the formal party.

22 I'm going to wear my new blue and white _ _ _ _ _ _ _ shirt today.

23 The cake has to bake in the _ _ _ _ for one hour before it's done.

24 Your _ _ _ _ _ is empty. Why don't you have some more food?

25 She just bought an expensive new pair of knee-high leather _ _ _ _ _ _.

2 At play

2.1 Sports

Words in context   _Read the following passage and do the exercises._

The first modern Olympic games were held in Athens in 1896. There were nine sports: **cycling, tennis, gymnastics, swimming, track and field, weight-lifting, rowing, wrestling** and **shooting. Sailing** was also to have taken place, but had to be canceled because of bad weather at sea. At that time, as today, most people were interested in the track and field events in the main stadium.

In the first Olympics there were no real team sports. Then, slowly, a few team sports joined the program. **Soccer** and **field hockey** were the first team sports introduced into the Olympics in London in 1908. Then in 1936, at the Berlin Olympics, the Germans brought in **handball** and the Americans had **basketball** accepted as an Olympic sport.

It often happens that the country that introduces a new sport into the Olympics then goes on to win the gold medals. In 1904, at the Olympics in St. Louis, the Americans introduced **boxing** and won all seven events. Five **horseback-riding** events were introduced into the 1912 Stockholm Olympics, and

Swedish riders won four of them. And in 1964, at the Tokyo Olympics, two sports which are very popular in Japan were introduced: **judo** and **volleyball**. The Japanese won all three gold medals in judo, and also won the first women's volleyball competition.

Some new sports have recently been added to the Olympics. In Los Angeles, in 1984, **baseball** was introduced and **windsurfing** became an Olympic sport. In Seoul, Korea, in 1988, there was **table tennis** for the first time, and tennis returned as an Olympic sport. Unlike tennis, some sports, such as **golf** and **rugby**, have been tried in the Olympics but have never returned.

The Olympic games continue to get bigger and bigger. They also get more and more expensive. Now many people are asking the questions: Are the Olympics too big? Will the Olympics continue? Should the Olympics continue?

Exercise 1

Complete the following chart from the information in the passage above. For each sport fill in the year and place it was first introduced into the Olympics.

1. YEAR_____ PLACE_____
2. YEAR_____ PLACE_____
3. YEAR_____ PLACE_____
4. YEAR_____ PLACE_____
5. YEAR_____ PLACE_____
6. YEAR_____ PLACE_____
7. YEAR_____ PLACE_____
8. YEAR_____ PLACE_____
9. YEAR_____ PLACE_____

Exercise 2

Put each of these sports into one of the three groups.

volleyball	golf	judo	handball	table tennis	tennis
sailing	swimming	cycling	boxing	soccer	basketball

sports played in teams	sports that can be played against one other person	sports that can be played alone
_____	_____	_____
_____	_____	_____
_____	_____	_____
_____	_____	_____

Exercise 3

Look at the pictures of sports equipment. Then write the name of the sport in which it is used under the appropriate picture.

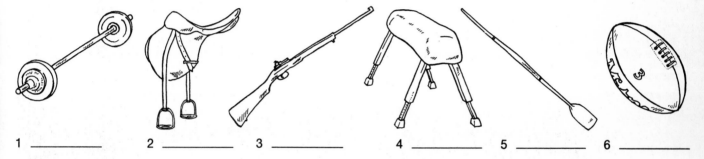

1 _____ 2 _____ 3 _____ 4 _____ 5 _____ 6 _____

Just for fun

Which sport is different from the other three in each group? There may be more than one possible answer, so discuss your answers with someone else.

1 a) basketball   b) soccer   c) tennis   d) baseball

2 a) judo   b) volleyball   c) boxing   d) wrestling

3 a) table tennis b) cycling   c) swimming   d) skiing

4 a) tennis   b) volleyball   c) table tennis d) basketball

5 a) baseball   b) golf   c) tennis   d) soccer

6 a) swimming   b) sailing   c) windsurfing   d) rowing

Think about

1 Which sports are you best at? How good are you? How long have you been playing? How often do you play?

2 Do you support a particular team? Which one? How often do you go to a sports event, or do you prefer to watch sports on television?

3 Which sports would you like to learn and why?

4 Do you think the Olympics should continue?

2.2 Actions in sports

Here are some rules taken from a few sports.

Words in context

Read the passages and do the exercises.

Tennis

After **throwing** the ball up in the air while **serving**, the player's feet must not come down inside the line of the tennis court until he or she has **hit** the ball. As soon as the ball hits the tennis racket, however, the server can **run** into the court ready to receive the return.

Football

When the quarterback* **passes** the ball to one of his players, the player on the other team who is trying to stop the receiver* from **catching** the ball is not allowed to **tackle** the receiver until the ball touches the receiver's hands. If he tackles too early, he has **committed a foul**. The next play begins where the foul took place.

*A quarterback and a receiver are players on a football team.

Soccer

When there is a penalty**, the goalkeeper must have both feet on the goal line and must not move until the player taking the penalty **kicks** the ball. If the goalkeeper starts to **dive** before the ball is touched, then the penalty has to be taken again.

**A penalty is a kick that a player takes from 12 yards in front of the goal after a foul has been committed inside a certain area.

Basketball

After a player **shoots** the ball, nobody is allowed to **jump** and stop the ball from going into the basket if the ball is on its way down into the basket. If this happens, even though the ball has not gone into the basket, the shooting team **scores** two points.

Exercise 1

Look at these pictures and decide if any of the players is breaking one of the rules. Write "OK" if no rule is broken, and "Not OK" if a rule is broken.

1 _____

3 _____

2 _____

4 _____

Exercise 2

Match each action with one of the definitions below.

a) jump	b) serve	c) kick	d) dive	e) shoot	f) pass	g) tackle	h) commit a foul

1 _____ send (the ball) to another player

2 _____ do something against the rules of the game

3 _____ throw yourself forwards or sideways

4 _____ begin playing for a new point

5 _____ try to get a point or goal

6 _____ take both feet off the ground

7 _____ stop someone from continuing (with the ball)

8 _____ hit with your foot

Exercise 3

Answer these questions with the names of sports from the list on the right.

In which sports . . .?

1 do you pass a ball from one player to another? _____ _____ _____ _____   a) tennis

2 do you hit a ball (but not with hands or feet)? _____ _____ _____   b) soccer

3 do you score goals? _____ _____   c) table tennis

4 do you have to jump to catch the ball? _____ _____   d) golf

5 do you have to serve? _____ _____ _____   e) basketball

6 do you have to shoot? _____ _____   f) volleyball

7 do you win by having the lowest score? _____   g) football

8 do you have to tackle? _____ _____

Dictionary work

Match the sports terms in the box with an appropriate definition. Do as many as you can and then check your answers in the dictionary.

a) referee	c) bat	e) set	g) match
b) tournament	d) course	f) umpire	h) stadium

1 _____ a complete game of tennis

2 _____ a place where golf is played

3 _____ games played to find the best team

4 _____ person who judges a game of tennis

5 _____ person who judges a game of football

6 _____ something used to hit a ball

7 _____ place where big sports events take place

8 _____ part of a game of tennis or table tennis

Think about

1 Think of your favorite sport. Are there any rules you would like to change? What are they and why?

2 Think of a particular sport and describe the qualities that a good player of that sport needs to have.

3 Which sports do you think are the most dangerous and why?

2.3 Party time

▪▪

A young man comes up to a young woman at a party and asks her to dance.

HIM: Hi. Would you like to dance?

HER: Sure. I'd love to.

HIM: Great party, isn't it? Are you **enjoying yourself**?

HER: Yes, I'm **having a very good time**.

HIM: Who's **giving** this **party**, anyway?

HER: You mean, you weren't **invited**? You're **crashing** the party?

HIM: No, not really. I came with a friend. He was invited.

HER: Oh, I see. Well, you see that girl over there. That's Jane. We're **celebrating** her eighteenth birthday.

HIM: Oh, it's a birthday party. Great. Did you give Jane a **present**?

HER: Of course. I gave her several **gifts**. By the way, where's your friend? Maybe I know him.

HIM: Let me see. There he is. See that guy sitting there all alone?

HER: He doesn't look as if he's **having** much **fun**.

HIM: No, he never enjoys parties. He always finds them **boring**.

HER: You two are very different then, eh?

HIM: Yeah. I love parties. You can **go wild** and do crazy things. And you can meet the most **exciting**, interesting people, like you.

HER: Well, thank you and thanks for the dance. Nice meeting you.

HIM: Don't you want to dance some more?

HER: Sorry. I can't. I have to go now and put the candles on Jane's cake. You see, I'm Jane's mother.

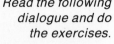

Words in context

Read the following dialogue and do the exercises.

Exercise 1

The following story describes what happened at the party. Fill in each blank with one word taken from the dialogue.

At a birthday (1)_____ a young man asked a young lady to (2)_____. She accepted.

While they were dancing he asked her if she was (3)_____ herself. She said she was. When he asked

her if she knew whose party it was, the woman asked him if he had been (4)_____. He explained that he

had come with a (5)_____ who had been invited. The lady then told him that the party was to

(6)_____ the birthday of a girl called Jane. The lady wanted to see who the young man's friend

was. He pointed to a boy sitting alone. The boy didn't look as if he was having (7)_____. The lady said

that the two friends were very (8)_____. The young man agreed, saying that his friend always found

parties (9)_____, but he liked to have a good time and do wild and (10)_____ things.

When the music stopped, the lady thanked him for the dance. The young man was upset and wanted to know why she

didn't want to dance any more. The lady then explained that she had to put some candles on Jane's birthday

(11)_____. She said she was Jane's (12)_____.

Exercise 2

Decide if the following pairs of words are similar in meaning or different. If you think
they are similar, write S in the blank space. If you think they are different, write D.

1 boring ———— exciting

2 enjoy yourself ———— have a good time

3 party ———— celebration

4 crash a party ———— be invited

5 wild ———— crazy

6 celebrate ———— invite

7 present ———— gift

8 be bored ———— be boring

9 have fun ———— enjoy yourself

10 candle ———— cake

Just for fun

Arrange the perfect party. Choose one possibility from each row and arrange the type of
party that you usually enjoy best.

night of the week	Mon	Tues	Wed	Thur	Fri	Sat	Sun			
starting time	2pm	4pm	6pm	7pm	8pm	9pm	10pm	12pm		
hours	1	2	3	4	5	6	7	8	9	10	11	12
main activity	talking	dancing	playing games	eating	watching TV/a movie					
number of men	0	1	2	4	8	10	15	20	25	40	60	100
number of women	0	1	2	4	8	10	15	20	25	40	60	100
type of music	none	rock	jazz	live music						
type of food	none	sandwiches	potato chips and pretzels	a real meal						
type of drink	none	coffee	soda	beer	wine					

Now compare your answers with someone else. See if you can find someone whose
answers show that they would like to come to your party!

Think about

1 On what different occasions do people have parties in your country?

2 What do people do at birthday parties in your country?

3 What do people do at New Year's Eve parties in your country?

4 When someone invites you to their home, do you usually take a gift with you? If so, what?

2.4 Places to go and things to do

Words in context

Read the following passage and do the exercises.

Luz is talking on the telephone to her friend Marge, a woman with two children. You only read Luz's side of the conversation, but try to imagine what Marge is saying.

"Hi, Marge. . . Yeah, it's me, Luz. _(a)_ Fine, and you?. . . Good. Listen. I'm just calling to see what you and the kids would like to do tomorrow. You're still coming over, aren't you?. . . Well, I thought we could **take a trip** somewhere. . . Oh, I don't know. Drive into the country and **go for a walk**. _(b)_ No? Well, would you like to be a tourist for the day and **go sightseeing** in the city? _(c)_ Oh, you think you've **seen** all **the sights**. . . Well, since you're bringing the kids, maybe we should go to the **circus** or to the **zoo**. There's a new baby elephant that was just born. _(d)_ The kids are too old for that, you think. Well, are they interested in visiting a **museum** or an **art gallery**? There's a very good **exhibit** of nineteenth-century French painting. _(e)_ No? Boring, huh?. . . Well, what do you think you would all like to do?. . . I see. You want to **go window-shopping**. _(f)_ No, that's fine with me. I don't mind at all. . . No, I'm sure. But what about the evening? I thought we could **go out to dinner**. _(g)_ No, I thought the kids could **stay at home** and watch television. . . Well, I thought we could also go to the **movies**. _(h)_ Really? How about some music? A **concert**? _(i)_ No. The **ballet** or the **opera**?. . . No? The **theater** to see a play?. . . No. Well, what do you want to do in the evening? _(j)_ You'd like to go to a **rock club** and dance. . . Um, yes, well, no, I just remembered that I promised to visit my mother tomorrow. . . Yes, what a shame. Another time maybe. . . Well, bye. Love to the kids."

Exercise 1

Find the places in the telephone conversation above where Marge said the following.

1 _____ "I don't think I feel like listening to music."

2 _____ "Do you mind?"

3 _____ "The kids are much too old for the circus and the zoo."

4 _____ "How are you?"

5 _____ "I'd like to go listen to some rock music and dance."

6 _____ "Would we take the children with us to the restaurant?"

7 _____ "I don't want to go to the country."

8 _____ "There's no movie that I really want to see at the moment."

9 _____ "I've been sightseeing there plenty of times."

10 _____ "No, I'm sure the kids don't want to go to any museum or art gallery."

Exercise 2

Fill in the following sentences with the most likely preposition (on, to, for, etc.) and/or article (a, an, the). When no article or preposition is necessary, write 0 in the blank.

1 Let's go _____ club.

2 Let's go _____ sightseeing.

3 Let's visit _____ museum.

4 Let's go _____ shopping.

5 Let's go _____ walk.

6 Let's take _____ trip.

7 Let's go _____ movies.

8 Let's go out _____ dinner.

9 Let's see _____ sights of Paris.

10 Let's stay _____ home.

Exercise 3

Why would you go to these places? Match each place with the most likely reason for going there.

a) a club	b) an art gallery	c) a concert	d) a theater	e) a zoo	f) a ballet

1 _____ to see a play

2 _____ to watch people dancing

3 _____ to dance

4 _____ to look at the animals

5 _____ to listen to music

6 _____ to look at paintings

Dictionary work

Where are you most likely to be if you can see the following people and things? Write your answers in the spaces below. Do as many as you can and then check your answers in the dictionary.

a) cages	d) a disc jockey	g) waiters
b) clowns	e) an orchestra	h) an exhibit
c) ballerinas	f) a big screen	i) a stage

1 _____ at the theater

2 _____ at the movies

3 _____ at the ballet

4 _____ at the circus

5 _____ at the zoo

6 _____ in a restaurant

7 _____ in a rock club

8 _____ in an art gallery

9 _____ at a concert

Think about

1 How often do you go out in the evenings? What do you usually do?

2 How much does it cost to go to the movies, the theater, the ballet and the opera in your country in the major cities?

3 Do you enjoy going to rock clubs? Why? Why not?

4 When you visit a new city, do you like to go sightseeing?

2.5 Time for a laugh

Words in context *Read the passage and do the questions.*

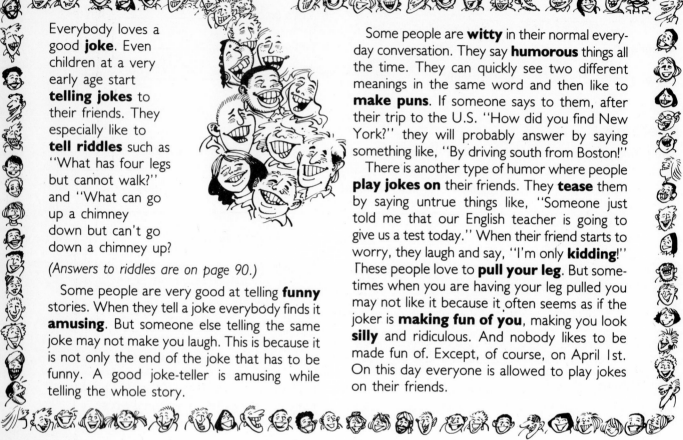

Everybody loves a good **joke**. Even children at a very early age start **telling jokes** to their friends. They especially like to **tell riddles** such as "What has four legs but cannot walk?" and "What can go up a chimney down but can't go down a chimney up?

(Answers to riddles are on page 90.)

Some people are very good at telling **funny** stories. When they tell a joke everybody finds it **amusing**. But someone else telling the same joke may not make you laugh. This is because it is not only the end of the joke that has to be funny. A good joke-teller is amusing while telling the whole story.

Some people are **witty** in their normal everyday conversation. They say **humorous** things all the time. They can quickly see two different meanings in the same word and then like to **make puns**. If someone says to them, after their trip to the U.S. "How did you find New York?" they will probably answer by saying something like, "By driving south from Boston!"

There is another type of humor where people **play jokes on** their friends. They **tease** them by saying untrue things like, "Someone just told me that our English teacher is going to give us a test today." When their friend starts to worry, they laugh and say, "I'm only **kidding**!" These people love to **pull your leg**. But sometimes when you are having your leg pulled you may not like it because it often seems as if the joker is **making fun of you**, making you look **silly** and ridiculous. And nobody likes to be made fun of. Except, of course, on April 1st. On this day everyone is allowed to play jokes on their friends.

Exercise 1

Use these words to fill in the blanks according to the information in the passage.

kidding	witty	friendly	riddles
joke	silly	true	amusing

1 Children particularly like to tell each other _____.

2 A riddle is a question that has an _____ and unexpected answer.

3 A good _____ is often a good story with a funny ending.

4 A _____ person is someone who says humorous things during a conversation.

5 When you pull someone's leg you may try to make them believe things which are not _____.

6 When you tell someone that you have been pulling their leg, you may say, "I was just _____".

7 One way of teasing someone is to pull their leg in a _____ way.

8 When you make fun of someone, you might make them do, say or believe something which makes them look

_____.

Exercise 2

Which words can go into sentence A and which into sentence B?

1 witty   _____

2 amusing   _____

3 joke   _____   **A** That was a very _____ thing that you said.

4 riddle   _____   **B** That was a very funny _____ .

5 humorous   _____

6 pun   _____

Exercise 3

Read the sentences below and say what each speaker is doing.

> a) telling a joke   b) making a pun   c) telling a riddle
> d) pulling someone's leg   e) making fun of another person

1 _____ "What is always coming but never arrives?" *(Answer on page 90)*

2 _____ "I've just heard your name on the radio. They said you just won first prize in the lottery."

3 _____ "Sunday is the strongest day of the week, because all the other days are weekdays."

4 _____ "A patient went to see his doctor because he had lost his memory. The doctor asked him, 'How long have you had this problem?' The patient answered, 'How long have I had what problem?' "

5 _____ "It was a very good movie, full of ideas and very clever, so there's no point in you going to see it."

Just for fun

Read this joke.

A man walking in the park found a monkey.

He took it to a policeman and asked him what he should do.

"Take it to the zoo," the policeman told him.

The next day the policeman saw the man still with the monkey.
"I thought I told you to take that monkey to the zoo," said the policeman.

"I did," said the man. "And today I'm taking it to the beach."

Now you tell a joke or a funny story.

Think about

1 What are some different types of a) jokes b) humor?

2 Is there a day in your country when you are expected to pull someone's leg?
  What sort of things do you do?

3 Who is your favorite comedian? Why?

Vocabulary review

2 At play (Units 2.1–2.5)

2.1 Sports
baseball
basketball
boxing
cycling
field hockey
football
golf
gymnastics
handball
horseback riding
judo
rowing
rugby
sailing
shooting
soccer
swimming
table tennis
tennis
track and field
volleyball
weightlifting
windsurfing
wrestling

2.2 Actions in sports
bat
catch
course
dive
foul
  commit a foul
jump
kick
match
pass
referee
run
score
serve
set
shoot
stadium
tackle
throw
tournament
umpire

2.3 Party time
bored
boring
celebrate
crash a party
enjoy (yourself)
exciting
fun
  have fun
gift
  give a gift
go wild
good time
  have a good time
invite
party
  give a party
present
  give a present

2.4 Place to go and things to do
art gallery
ballerina
ballet
cage
circus
clown
club
  rock club
concert
dinner
  go out to dinner
disc jockey
exhibit
museum
opera
orchestra
screen
sights
  see the sights
sightseeing
  go sightseeing
stage
stay at home
theater
trip
  take a trip

waiter
walk
  go for a walk
window-shopping
  go window-shopping
zoo

2.5 Time for a laugh
amusing
fun
  make fun of
funny
humorous
joke
  play a joke on
  tell a joke
kid
  be kidding
pull someone's leg
pun
  make a pun
riddle
  tell a riddle
silly
tease
witty

Test yourself 3

Use the words from the **Vocabulary review** to help you fill in the blanks in these sentences. The number of dashes corresponds to the number of letters in the missing word. More than one answer may be possible but there is always one best answer.

1 I hate it when people _ _ _ _ _ me. I think they are making fun of me.

2 I'd like to go on a _ _ _ _ _ _ _ _ _ _ _ _ tour of all the capital cities of Europe.

3 I don't want to go anywhere this weekend. I just want to _ _ _ _ at home.

4 In the last basketball game I _ _ _ _ _ _ sixteen points.

5 In this theater the _ _ _ _ _ is in the middle and the audience sits all around it.

6 How many people did you _ _ _ _ _ _ to the party?

7 You didn't really get married yesterday, did you? Come on, you're _ _ _ _ _ _ _ , aren't you?

8 My cousin has started _ _ _ _ _ _ _ _ _ _ _ _ _ . He wants to build up his muscles.

9 Our team reached the final of the _ _ _ _ _ _ _ _ _ _ by winning six matches.

10 Did you think that _ _ _ _ was funny? I couldn't understand it.

11 It helps to be tall if you want to play _ _ _ _ _ _ _ _ _ _ .

12 Let's take a _ _ _ _ to the country this weekend.

13 How many birthday _ _ _ _ _ _ _ _ did you get this year?

14 She's so _ _ _ _ _ _ . Sometimes when I'm talking to her I just can't stop laughing.

15 In both tennis and volleyball you are not allowed to touch the _ _ _ during the game.

16 "Did you _ _ _ _ _ your vacation?"
"Yes, very much."

17 Do you think _ _ _ _ _ _ _ is more difficult in the ocean or on a lake?

18 How do you _ _ _ _ _ _ _ _ _ the New Year in your country?

19 You should read this. It's very _ _ _ _ _ _ _ _ . I think you'll laugh.

20 He gave up playing football, but continued his interest in the sport by becoming a _ _ _ _ _ _ _ _ .

21 There's a very interesting exhibit at the _ _ _ _ _ _ this month.

22 The soccer player received the ball in front of the goal and everyone shouted, "_ _ _ _ _ _ !"

23 It was a very _ _ _ _ _ _ football game. The final score was 3–0.

24 _ _ _ _ _ _ _ _ _ _ can be a very beautiful sport to watch. It's almost like ballet dancing.

25 Mark tried to _ _ _ _ _ _ the ball but he missed, and it broke a window.

2.6 Entertainers

Words in context *Read the following passages and do the exercises.*

Have you ever stood in front of a large group of people and had to speak or perform? Some people perform in front of an audience every single day. They are the professional **entertainers** and their work is not always easy.

Every night in the theater, **actors** and **actresses** have to remember thousands of words. Every night in concert halls and night clubs, **musicians** try hard to make no mistakes when they play their music. **Singers** worry about singing the right notes. **Magicians** are nervous about making mistakes, worrying that one day a magic trick or a card trick will not work. Circus **clowns** and night club **comedians**, however, may have the hardest job of all. They have to make people laugh every day with well-told jokes and funny acts. No, being an entertainer is not such an easy way to make a living.

A lot of people also think that all entertainers are well paid, but not everyone in the entertainment world makes a lot of money. Of course, there are a few **movie stars, rock stars** and **television personalities** who make millions of dollars every time they open their mouths. There are also a few famous **movie directors** who make a lot of money telling actors and actresses how to speak and where to stand. Some of the best **stunt men** and **women** are also well paid for jumping out of moving cars and off high buildings, and for all the other dangerous things that they have to do. However, there are also thousands and thousands of actors, actresses and singers who find it very difficult to get work acting and singing. Then, when they do find work, most of them earn very little money.

Exercise 1

Decide if the following statements are true (T) or false (F) according to the information in the passage.

1 _____ An audience is a group of people who watch a performer.

2 _____ Actors and actresses have to have good memories.

3 _____ Many performers worry that something may go wrong.

4 _____ Clowns and comedians don't want their audiences to laugh.

5 _____ It is easy to make money as an entertainer.

6 _____ The best-paid entertainers are, in fact, not very famous.

7 _____ Stunt men and women can make a lot of money.

8 _____ Although many actors are unemployed, they are usually well paid when they are working.

Exercise 2

Match each picture to a person working in the entertainment industry.

movie director	actress	magician	stunt man	clown

1 _____ 2 _____ 3 _____ 4 _____ 5 _____

Exercise 3

Match each entertainer with a description of his or her work.

1 A comedian _____

2 A movie star _____

3 An actor _____

4 A musician _____

5 A rock star _____

6 A magician _____

7 A stunt woman _____

a) does clever tricks with his or her hands.

b) makes records.

c) has an important part in a movie.

d) tells jokes.

e) does dangerous things.

f) plays in an orchestra, group or band.

g) performs in plays on the stage.

Just for fun

Take any letter of the alphabet. Then see how quickly you can find a famous person to fill each box in the chart. Each person's last name must begin with the same letter. See if you can fill in the chart more quickly than your friends.

Each name will begin with the letter _____

1 a comedian	
2 a male rock star	
3 a female pop star	
4 a movie director	
5 a famous male movie star	
6 a famous female movie star	

Think about

1 Have you ever performed? What did you do? Did you enjoy doing it?

2 Would you like to be famous like a movie star or a rock star? Why? Why not?

3 Who are your favorite movie stars, rock stars, comedians and television personalities?

4 What magic tricks can you perform?

2.7 Music

Concerts at the GLENWOOD ARTS CENTER

Words in context
Read the passages and then do the exercises.

June 22nd LAS PALOMAS — This South American **group** plays the traditional **tunes** and sings the popular **folk** songs of Peru and Bolivia.

June 30th THE BAD BAD BOYS  — **Punk rock** from one of the new wave of **bands** coming out of London.

July 7th RONNIE PARQUETTE — One of the world's greatest **jazz** musicians excites you with the wonderful **rhythms** of his **saxophone**.

July 14th "ELVIS LIVES!" — He looks like Elvis! He sings like Elvis! Jimmy Wilkes creates the great sound of the King of **rock 'n 'roll**—Elvis Presley.

July 19th AN EVENING OF CLASSICAL MUSIC — The Vienna Orchestra plays some of your favorite works — the timeless **melodies** of Mozart, Strauss and Beethoven.

July 22nd JAMAICA INN — This West Indian band plays **reggae** music that will make you want to get up and dance. Listen and dance to the great reggae **beat**.

July 28th "SIXTIES NIGHT!" — **Rock** music from the 1960s played by *Sam and the Band*. Remember the songs and sounds of the greats — the Beatles, the Beach Boys, the Hollies and many, many more.

Exercise 1

Match the names of the performers with the type of music that they play.

1 _____ The Bad Bad Boys	a) rock 'n' roll music
2 _____ Jimmy Wilkes	b) jazz
3 _____ Jamaica Inn	c) punk rock
4 _____ Las Palomas	d) classical music
5 _____ The Vienna Orchestra	e) reggae
6 _____ Ronnie Parquette	f) folk music

Exercise 2

Which drawings represent the words below?

| band rhythm tune melody beat group |

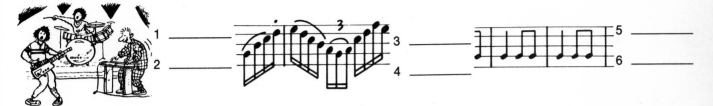

Exercise 3

Complete this chart by putting an X next to the characteristics of each type of music.

	rock 'n' roll	punk rock	folk	reggae	jazz	classical
1 often played by a big orchestra in a concert hall						
2 often played by young people with guitars in a group						
3 often played by young people with brightly colored hair						
4 often simple tunes which are popular for a short time						
5 music coming originally from Afro-American musicians						
6 music of a specific region, popular for a very long time						
7 music with a strong regular rhythm, originally from Jamaica						
8 music which is popular for dancing in rock clubs						
9 often played freely, not following written music						

Dictionary work

Match the names of the musical instruments to the pictures.

a) guitar   b) organ   c) saxophone   d) violin   e) piano   f) trumpet   g) flute   h) drums

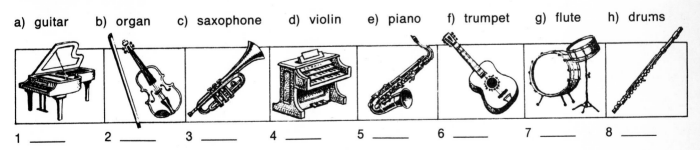

1 _____   2 _____   3 _____   4 _____   5 _____   6 _____   7 _____   8 _____

Think about

1 What type of music do you most like to listen to when you are a) with friends
   b) relaxing alone c) dancing? What about your parents' generation?

2 Do you play a musical instrument? How long have you played? How well do you play?

3 What is a new popular type of music at the moment? Can you describe it?

2.8 Television

Words in context   *Read about the television programs on Monday evening on Channels 1, 2 and 3 and then do the exercises.*

	Channel 1		Channel 2		Channel 3	
7:00	**The News**	With Janet Chung.	**The Million Dollar Minute**	A **documentary** about **commercials** which can cost $1 million during prime time TV.	**Globe**	Nightly **soap opera** that takes you into the lives and loves of people on a major San Francisco newspaper.
7:30	**Name that Movie**	the popular weekly **game show** in which contestants show how much they know about the movies.			**World News on Monday**	Alice Tamms and John Johnson bring you the latest news from around the world.
8:00	**Movie of the Week**	Jaws (1975). Movie about a shark that terrorizes a small tourist resort.	**(7:45) Chicago Cops**	New **detective series** set in Chicago. McTaggart and Smith are the two cops who fight crime in the windy city.	**Life with Susan**	The first of a new weekly **comedy** series about a father who lives alone with his daughter Susan.
8:30					**Tom and Jerry**	More comedy with a half-hour of **cartoons**, showing your favorite cat and mouse.
9:00			**(8:45) News and Weather**	With Arthur Small.		
			Sport on Two	The **sports show** that takes you back to some of the greatest moments in sports history. Tonight: Superbowl XIII.	**Night of Death**	1987 movie made for television. A killer goes crazy in New York's subway.
9:30	**Night Time**	The nightly **current affairs** program hosted by Gordon Foster, who looks at the latest in world events.				
10:00	**Tennis**	The best match from today's play at the Paris Open Tennis Torunament.			**Face to Face**	In Roger Baltham's **talk show** this week he interviews the movie star Gloria Braggio.

Exercise 1

On which channels can you watch the following types of program on Monday evening?

1 a sports show	a) 1 & 2	b) 2 & 3	c) 1 & 3	d) 1, 2, & 3
2 the news	a) 1 & 2	b) 2 & 3	c) 1 & 3	d) 1, 2, & 3
3 a comedy show	a) 1	b) 2	c) 3	d) 1, 2, & 3
4 a movie	a) 1	b) 1 & 2	c) 1 & 3	d) 1, 2, & 3
5 a game show	a) 1	b) 2	c) 3	d) 2 & 3
6 a detective series	a) 1	b) 2	c) 3	d) 1 & 2
7 a current affairs program	a) 1	b) 2	c) 3	d) 1 & 3
8 a talk show	a) 1	b) 2	c) 3	d) 2 & 3

Exercise 2

What type of television program are you probably watching if you see the following?
Match the descriptions on the left with the programs on the right.

1 _____ People trying to answer questions

2 _____ Actors doing and saying funny things

3 _____ People discussing politics

4 _____ The animal life of Antarctica

5 _____ Guns, murder and police

6 _____ A long interview with a famous person

7 _____ The everyday lives of the same group of people

8 _____ Characters played by moving drawings, not people

9 _____ Someone talking about a new soap powder

10 _____ A person telling you what happened today

a) a detective series

b) a commercial

c) a soap opera

d) a comedy series

e) a talk show

f) a current affairs program

g) a nature documentary

h) the news

i) a game show

j) a cartoon

Just for fun

Imagine you can choose the programs to go on two television channels in the evening. Fill in the chart below with the names of the television programs and say what types they are (news, sports, talk show, etc.)

	CHANNEL 4	CHANNEL 11
7:00	_____	_____
8:00	_____	_____
9:00	_____	_____
10:00	_____	_____

Think about

1 How much time do you spend watching television? What are your favorite types of programs?

2 How many hours a day is television on in your country? How many different television channels are there? What is the difference between them?

3 What are the good and bad things about television?

2.9 Reading

Words in context *Read the following passage and do the exercises.*

Some people think that as more and more people have televisions in their homes, fewer and fewer people will buy **books** and **newspapers**. Why read an **article** in the newspaper, when the TV news can bring you the information in a few minutes and with pictures? Why read a **novel**, when a **play** on television can tell you the same story with color, picture and action?

Why read the **biographies** of famous men and women, when an hour-long television program can tell you all that you want to know? Television has not killed **reading**, however. Today, newspapers and **magazines** sell in very large numbers. And books of every kind are sold more than ever before. Books are still a cheap way to get information and entertainment. Although some books with hard covers are expensive, many books are published today as **paperbacks**, which are reasonably cheap. A paperback novel, for example, is always cheaper than an evening at the movies or the theater, and you can keep a book forever and read it many times.

Books in the home are a wonderful source of knowledge and pleasure and some types of books should be in every home. Every home should have a good **dictionary**. Every home should have an **atlas** of the world, with large clear maps. It might be expensive, but a good **encyclopedia** is useful, too, because you can find information on any subject. In addition, it is useful to have on your bookshelves other **non-fiction** books such as history books, science **textbooks**, cook books, books about medicine and health, etc. It is equally important to have some **fiction** on your shelves, too. Then you can relax with a good **story**, or from time to time you can take a book of **poems** off your shelves and read the thoughts and feelings of your favorite poets.

Exercise 1

Choose the best answer according to the information in the passage.

1 Which is easier to get the news from?
   a) a newspaper   b) the television

2 Which is usually quicker?
   a) to read a biography of a famous person
   b) to watch a television program about a famous person

3 Which is usually cheaper?
   a) a paperback   b) an evening at the movies

4 Which is usually cheaper?
   a) a paperback   b) a hard cover book

5 Which is it most important to have in your home?
   a) non-fiction books, such as a dictionary and an encyclopedia
   b) fiction, such as novels, short stories and books of poems
   c) a mixture of both good non-fiction and your favorite fiction

Exercise 2

Which of the following are non-fiction and which are fiction? Put the words into the appropriate column.

| atlas | novel | short story | textbook | play | dictionary | encyclopedia | poem |

fiction	**non-fiction**
_____	_____
_____	_____
_____	_____
_____	_____

Exercise 3

Match the words on the left with their definitions on the right.

1 _____ an article

2 _____ an atlas

3 _____ a biography

4 _____ a novel

5 _____ a textbook

6 _____ a dictionary

7 _____ a poem

8 _____ a paperback

9 _____ a magazine

a) a book that is used to study a school subject

b) a publication that comes out weekly or monthly

c) a book with maps of the world

d) usually a cheap book with a soft cover

e) a story about a real person

f) a piece of writing in a newspaper

g) a book of word definitions

h) usually a short piece of writing expressing a deep feeling or thought

i) a story about people who are not real

Dictionary work

Decide if the following words usually have to do with newspapers or textbooks. Write (N) next to the newspaper words and (T) next to the textbook words. Do as many as you can and then check your answers in the dictionary.

1 _____ bibliography

2 _____ column

3 _____ chapter

4 _____ headline

5 _____ title

6 _____ classified ads

7 _____ crossword puzzle

8 _____ cartoon

9 _____ appendix

10 _____ glossary

11 _____ editorial

12 _____ introduction

Think about

1 What newspapers and magazines are there in your country? Describe them.

2 What type of books do you like to read? Who are your favorite writers?

3 How many books do you read in a year? How many do you buy?

2.10 The art of conversation

Words in context *Read the passages and do the exercises.*

Alex and Chris love to **chat** for hours on the telephone. Their favorite topic is their neighbors. Here is an example of the two of them **gossiping** on the telephone. "Did you see the new couple who moved in next door to me? Do you think they're married? You know, last night they were **having** a terrible **argument**. They were **shouting** at each other so loud I could hear almost every word through the walls. He's very handsome, don't you think? And have you seen her car? It's so big. And you know something else, I think she's going to have a baby." (Now answer question 1, Exercise 1.)

For the fiftieth time in his life Professor Marchant stood up to **give a lecture** on the causes of World War I. He started, "Today I'm going to **discuss** with you the causes of World War I... Soon, as usual, most of the students were sleeping. The students who were awake could not take good notes, because they could only hear clearly one or two words in every sentence. You see, Marchant was not only boring, but he **mumbled** a great deal when he spoke. It was as if he always had mashed potatoes in his mouth when he was speaking. (Now answer question 2.)

For the first time in his life, Mr. Parrot had to **give a speech**. His daughter had just gotten married and there were a hundred guests at the wedding waiting to hear his words. He had practiced his speech for hours until he could say it perfectly and he had five pages of notes to help him. He stood up and started. "Th-th-th-th-thank you f-f-f-f-f c-c-c-c-coming," he **stuttered**, and then sat down very red in the face. (Now answer question 3.)

The two boys sat **whispering** to each other at the back of the classroom. In very quiet voices they were having a very interesting **conversation** about football, girls, parents and even school. Meanwhile, Mrs. Gomez talked and talked and talked about William Shakespeare. At the end of the lesson, Mrs. Gomez looked at the two boys and said, "Next time you have a conversation in my class, please don't whisper. Talk a little louder so that we can all enjoy what you are saying." (Now answer question 4.)

Exercise 1

Decide which is the best answer according to the information in the passages.

1 Alex and Chris love to talk about
   a) themselves
   b) people they know
   c) people in the news

2 None of the students could take good notes because
   a) they were sleeping
   b) the professor was boring
   c) the professor spoke unclearly

3 Mr. Parrot only said four words because
   a) he had prepared a short speech
   b) he was very nervous
   c) he always had problems saying the first letters of a word

4 The next time the boys were in her class, Mrs. Gomez really wanted them
   a) not to whisper   b) to talk more clearly
   c) not to have a conversation

Exercise 2

Match the situations with the most likely way of talking.

1 You are talking to someone in a library. You are _____

2 You and your friends are talking about politics. You are _____

3 Someone is talking in his sleep. He is _____

4 Your professor is telling you about the history of Europe. She is _____

5 The President is talking to the country on TV. He is _____

6 A parent is angry with her son. She is _____

7 You are disagreeing with your friend about politics. You are _____

8 Someone has trouble saying the first letters of some words. He is ____

9 You are talking with a friend about the weather. You are _____

10 Your neighbors are talking about your friends. They are _____

a) shouting
b) mumbling
c) chatting
d) gossiping
e) whispering
f) giving a lecture
g) discussing
h) having an argument
i) stuttering
j) giving a speech

Dictionary work

Match the sentences with their functions as in the example. Do as many as you can and then check your answers in the dictionary.

a) accuse	c) apologize	e) warn	g) advise	i) forgive	k) exaggerate
b) beg	d) confess	f) deny	h) promise	j) agree	l) threaten

Example: "Waiter, my soup is cold" Function: complain

1 _____ "It doesn't matter that you stole my book."

2 _____ "I didn't do it. I didn't steal any money."

3 _____ "I did it. I stole the money."

4 _____ "Please, please, please help me."

5 _____ "If you don't give me the money, I'll kill you."

6 _____ "I really think you ought to get a new job."

7 _____ "Be careful."

8 _____ "This is the worst, worst day in my whole life."

9 _____ "I will help you. I really will"

10 _____ "You did it. You stole the money."

11 _____ "You're right."

12 _____ "I'm sorry."

Think about

1 Have you ever given a speech? When? What was it about? Were you nervous?

2 What are the qualities of a good speaker or lecturer?

3 Do you have a lot of arguments in your family? What are they usually about?

4 What is the difference between a) a gossip and a conversation
b) a conversation and a discussion c) a discussion and an argument?

Vocabulary review

2 At play (Units 2.6–2.10)

2.6 Entertainers

actor
actress
clown
comedian
entertainer
magician
movie director
movie star
musician
rock star
singer
stunt man/woman
television personality

2.7 Music

band
beat
classical
drums
flute
folk
group
guitar
jazz
melody
orchestra
organ
piano
punk rock
reggae
rhythm
rock
rock 'n' roll
saxophone
trumpet
tune
violin

2.8 Television

advertisement
cartoon
channel
comedy
commercial
current affairs
detective stories
documentary
game show
movie
news
program
series
show
soap opera
talk show

2.9 Reading

appendix
article
atlas
bibliography
biography
book
cartoon
chapter
classified ad
column
crossword puzzle
dictionary
editorial
encyclopedia
fiction
glossary
headline
introduction
magazine
newspaper
non-fiction
novel
paperback
play
poem
story
textbook
title

2.10 The art of conversation

accuse
advise
agree
apologize
argument
   have an argument
beg
chat
confess
conversation
   have a conversation
deny
discuss
exaggerate
forgive
gossip
lecture
   give a lecture
mumble
promise
shout
speech
   give a speech
stutter
threaten
warn
whisper

Test yourself 4

Use the words from the **Vocabulary review** to help you fill in the blanks in these sentences. The number of dashes corresponds to the number of letters in the missing word. More than one answer may be possible but there is always one best answer.

1 When I want to relax, I really like to listen to eighteenth-century _ _ _ _ _ _ _ _ _ music.

2 I always wonder whether _ _ _ _ _ _ _ _ _ write their own jokes.

3 Turn on the _ _ _ _. I've just heard there's been a terrible plane crash.

4 I have no idea what to do next. Could you possibly _ _ _ _ _ _ me?

5 "Haven't you finished that novel I lent you?"
"Almost. I've just started the last _ _ _ _ _ _ _."

6 How many television _ _ _ _ _ _ _ _ do you have in your country?

7 When _ _ _ _ music first started, many parents didn't want their children to listen to it.

8 Is there a _ _ _ _ _ _ _ _ in that textbook? I can't find one at the back?

9 What was the name of the _ _ _ _ _ _ _ who played Lady Macbeth at the Globe Theater?

10 Do you get nervous when you have to give a _ _ _ _ _ _ in front of a lot of people?

11 Our band has a singer and three guitarists, but we still need someone to play the _ _ _ _ _ _.

12 He's one of the best _ _ _ _ _ _ _ _ _ I've ever seen. I've no idea how he does his tricks.

13 What's the _ _ _ _ _ _ _ _ on the front page of today's newspaper?

14 There's a new detective _ _ _ _ _ _ _ starting on television tomorrow night.

15 Good public speakers never _ _ _ _ _ _ _. They always speak very clearly.

16 Children all over the world have enjoyed the movies and cartoons of the great _ _ _ _-_ _ _ _ _ _ _ _ _, Walt Disney.

17 Most people think that Shakespeare only wrote plays, but he also wrote many wonderful _ _ _ _ _ _.

18 Last night there was a very interesting _ _ _ _ _ _ _ _ _ _ _ on television about mountain climbing.

19 "How important are the words in a rock song?"
"Not very. I think people most want a good _ _ _ _ to dance to."

20 If you don't want anyone else to hear, _ _ _ _ _ _ _ _ in my ear.

21 Children always love the circus and especially the _ _ _ _ _ _ _.

22 Who is the most popular _ _ _ _ _ _ in your country and what sort of music do they play?

23 I always like to _ _ _ _ with the person next to me on a long train or plane ride.

24 I couldn't find one interesting article in last month's _ _ _ _ _ _ _ _ _.

25 What sort of _ _ _ _ _ _ _ _ _ _ _ _ _ _ do you think are most effective in selling a company's product?

3 At work

3.1 Jobs

Words in context *Read the following passages and do the exercises.*

 My name is Martha Glass. I'm thirty-nine years old and I'm a **doctor**. I chose the medical **profession** because I wanted to help people and at the same time make good money. When I was younger I wanted to become a **teacher** or a **nurse**, but I soon realized there wasn't much money in either of those professions. My parents didn't help me much, because they didn't want me to have a **career** at all. They wanted me to do what so many other girls did. They wanted me to become a **secretary**, marry the **boss**, have kids and stay at home. Well, I got married, and I had kids, but I have my career as well.

 My name is George Dulek. I'm a **businessman**. I'm fifty years old and I've been working for the same company for twenty-five years. I think I've had a very successful career. I started work with the company as a poorly paid **clerk**. I was one of those nine-to-five **white-collar office workers** who spend all day with a pencil in one hand and a telephone in the other. I hated it. So I got transferred to sales and became one of the company's **sales representatives**. I traveled all over the country selling the company's products and became the most successful **salesperson** on the staff. Now I'm the **manager** of the sales department. In another ten years I hope to retire with a good pension.

 Hi. I'm Billy. I quit school when I was sixteen. I didn't have any qualifications. I just wanted to earn some money. I got a **job** in a factory. I didn't mind being a **blue-collar** worker. All I wanted was enough money to take my girlfriends out on a Saturday night. But then they got robots in to do my job and I was **out of work**. I was out of work for sixteen months. It's terrible being **unemployed**. The days seem so long. I finally got a job as an **unskilled** laborer, working for a builder. I'm twenty-five now. I suppose I should go to night school and get some extra training so that I can earn more money as a **skilled** worker.

Exercise 1

Answer the following questions according to the information in the passages.

	Martha	George	Billy	No one
1 Who had a white-collar job for a while?				
2 Who works in a profession?				
3 Who wanted to become a secretary?				
4 Who is unemployed at the moment?				
5 Who is an unskilled worker?				
6 Who was a successful salesperson?				
7 Who wanted a different career as a child?				
8 Who married the boss?				
9 Who has no career?				
10 Who was out of work for a while?				

Exercise 2

Find the words and phrases which are similar in meaning.

| blue-collar worker | factory worker | unemployed | boss |
| out of work | office worker | manager | white-collar worker |

1 _____ is similar in meaning to _____.

2 _____ is similar in meaning to _____.

3 _____ is similar in meaning to _____.

4 _____ is similar in meaning to _____.

Exercise 3

Decide what kinds of jobs the following are. Put an X in the correct box.	professional worker	white-collar worker	skilled worker
1 engineer			
2 secretary			
3 bank teller			
4 architect			
5 teacher			
6 mechanic			
7 lawyer			
8 computer repairperson			
9 office manager			
10 hairdresser			

Just for fun

What do you think is most important to you in a job and what is least important? Put the following in order (from 1 to 6). Discuss your answer with someone else and explain your order.

_____ flexible working hours   _____ contact with interesting people   _____ chance to travel

_____ long vacations   _____ nice, quiet, attractive work space   _____ a good pension

What are some other things that you think make a good job?

Think about

1 Have you ever had a job? How many? What kind were they?

2 What are some good jobs to have and why? What are the worst jobs?

3 Would you rather have an uninteresting well paid job or an interesting but poorly paid job?

4 Are there many unemployed people in your country? Who? Young? Old? People in the north or south? How can they find jobs?

3.2 Farm work

Words in context *Read the description of a typical year on a farm and then do the exercises.*

Spring is the time to prepare the soil for **planting**. First, the farmer **fertilizes** his **fields** with cow **manure** or a chemical fertilizer. Then he **plows** the soil, turning it over and mixing in the fertilizer to provide a rich soil for the **crops**. Later, when the days are a little longer and the sun has warmed the soil, it is time to plant the seeds. Meanwhile, if the farmer raises animals, spring is the time when the animals are giving birth, and both mothers and their young ones have to be watched and cared for.

After planting, the farmer waits and watches. He watches the weather, hoping for enough sun. He **waters** the young plants and watches carefully for signs of plant disease and the attacks of insects. Many farmers **spray** their fields with chemicals to keep away disease and harmful insects. With water, sun, care and protection the plants grow strong and healthy.

The days are getting shorter and shorter. The harvested crops are sold in the markets or **stored** in the **barns**, ready to **feed** the animals through the winter months. The farmer **chops** wood, preparing to keep his house warm through the long cold winter nights. And when winter finally comes, it is a time for planning, for deciding where and what to plant next year. For soon it will be spring again and the cycle of planting, growing and harvesting will start again.

This is the busiest time of the year. Now the crops in the fields are ready to **harvest**. The fruit is ready to **pick**. It is time to **gather** in the vegetable crops and to **reap** the grass crops, such as **wheat** and corn. The farmers have to work quickly. Often it is necessary to call in extra workers to work in their fields and bring in the crops. Work starts when the sun rises and finishes when the sun sets. The days are hard and long. But when the job is done, it is time for celebrating, for dancing, eating, drinking and having fun.

Exercise 1

Fill in the chart according to the information above. Decide whether a job is done on the farm in spring, summer, fall or winter.

		spring	summer	fall	winter
1	The fields are planted.				
2	The fruit is picked.				
3	The crops are sprayed.				
4	The corn is reaped.				
5	The fields are planned.				
6	The wood is chopped.				
7	The crops are stored in the barns.				
8	The fields are plowed.				
9	The fields are watered.				
10	The fields are fertilized.				

Exercise 2

Put these events in the order in which they usually occur.

1 First, the farmers _____

2 Then, they _____

3 After that, they _____

4 They may have to _____

5 Finally, it's time to _____

6 Then they have to _____

7 Now they can _____

a) harvest the crops.
b) fertilize their fields.
c) feed the animals in the winter.
d) store the crops.
e) plant the crops.
f) plow the fields.
g) spray the crops.

Exercise 3

Match the verbs on the left with each noun on the right in order to make a job that you are likely to find on a farm.

	the horses	the soil	the wood	the crops	the corn	the grapes	the chickens	the vegetables	the fields
plow									
harvest									
chop									
feed									
pick									
water									

Dictionary work

Match the words in the box with the definitions below.

a) a hen   c) a tractor   e) a bull   g) manure   i) a vineyard   k) a shepherd
b) a field   d) a barn   f) wheat   h) an ax   j) soil   l) cattle

1 _____ earth; the place where plants grow

2 _____ a sharp tool for chopping trees

3 _____ a male animal that can be dangerous

4 _____ a farm animal that lays eggs

5 _____ a person on a farm who looks after the sheep

6 _____ a powerful motor vehicle used on a farm

7 _____ a piece of land on a farm

8 _____ cows

9 _____ a grass crop, grown to make flour for bread

10 _____ a piece of land for growing grapes for wine

11 _____ animal waste used for fertilizer

12 _____ a farm building often used for storing crops

Think about

1 Have you ever visited a farm? When? Where? What did you do? What did you see?

2 Are farmers usually rich or poor in your country? What do they usually grow?

3 Would you like to be a farmer? Why? Why not?

3.3 Tools and their uses

Words in context   *Read the following passages and do the exercises.*

Imagine that you have two pieces of wood and some tools in your hands. How many different ways of joining them together can you think of? Before you read any further, spend a few moments trying to answer this question. *There are, in fact, many possible ways. Here are six.*

1 The simplest method of all is probably to take some **string** and **tie** one piece of wood to the other. This method will probably not keep the two pieces together for very long.

2 Another simple way is to take some wood **glue** and put it on both pieces of wood. You will have to press the two pieces together very hard and if you are lucky your two pieces will **stick** together.

3 Another way is to use **nails**. You'll need a **hammer**. Then bang the nails into the wood. The nails must not be too big or they will crack the wood. And they must not be too small or the wood will not stay together.

4 If you want to use **screws** to put the two pieces of wood together, you first have to **drill** a hole through one of the pieces. You also have to start a hole in the second piece of wood. Then push the screw through the first hole and use a **screwdriver** to **screw** it in until it is tightly in the second piece of wood. Using screws is usually a very strong way of joining two pieces of wood.

5 Instead of using screws you could use a **nut** and **bolt**. This time you have to drill a hole through both pieces of wood. Then you push the bolt through both holes and **tighten** a nut onto the end of the bolt using a **wrench**.

6 The most complicated way of joining two pieces of wood together is to make a joint. To do this you need a **saw**. There are many different types of joints, but the basic idea is to cut a shape in one piece of wood and to **saw** out a matching piece in the other piece of wood. Then you fit the two pieces together and stick them together with glue.

Exercise 1

Match the six different ways of joining wood together, described above (1–6), with the pictures below.

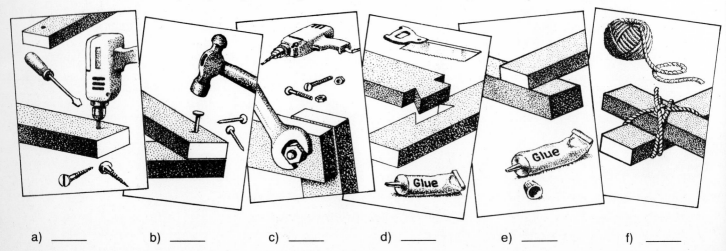

a) _____   b) _____   c) _____   d) _____   e) _____   f) _____

Exercise 2

Divide the following words into two groups: tools and things that are used with tools.

| screw | hammer | nail | glue | wrench | saw | bolt | screwdriver |

tools   **things used with tools**

_____   _____

_____   _____

_____   _____

_____   _____

Exercise 3

Complete the first half of the sentence on the left with the best phrase from the right.

1 She drilled _____   a) the piece of wood in two.

2 She sawed _____   b) the pieces of wood together with string.

3 She tightened _____   c) a nail.

4 She stuck _____   d) a hole in the piece of wood.

5 She tied _____   e) the pieces of wood together with glue.

6 She hammered in _____   f) the screw with a screwdriver.

Just for fun

The words on the right are hidden in the word find. Can you find them? If you do not know all the words, look them up in your dictionary.

K	P	S	R	E	I	L	P	O	P
S	N	R	C	F	I	N	K	I	R
N	A	I	L	R	I	F	H	K	I
A	R	W	A	R	E	S	A	N	L
D	E	O	D	E	C	W	M	H	L
E	N	D	D	E	M	K	A	I	L
P	A	A	E	G	N	M	I	D	I
S	P	E	R	I	M	M	L	R	R
S	I	R	F	E	E	X	I	E	D
W	R	E	R	I	W	E	R	S	C

saw
spade
pliers
hammer
screw
nail
ladder
wire
knife
drill

Think about

1 What advice would you give someone on how to use a hammer, a saw and a screwdriver?

2 Have you ever made anything with tools? What did you make? What tools did you use?

3 Do schools teach both boys and girls how to use tools in your country?

4 What are the basic tools that should be in every home?

3.4 Shopping

Words in context *Read the story and do the exercises.*

Exercise 1

Decide if the following statements are true (T) or false (F) according to the story.

1 _____ The man returned the television because it was broken.

2 _____ The man wanted a refund.

3 _____ The salesman offered him a credit.

4 _____ Every television in the store was reduced.

5 _____ The Zandy 3000 was being sold at half price.

6 _____ If the Zandy 3000 breaks in the next year, the man will get his money back.

7 _____ The Zandy 3000 cost more than the television that the man had returned.

8 _____ The man paid by check.

9 _____ The man bought the last Zandy 3000 in the store.

10 _____ The salesman was very good at his job.

Exercise 2

Decide if the following sentences are similar (S) or different (D) in meaning.

1 It's fifty percent off. _____ It's half price.

2 It's a bargain. _____ It's a good deal.

3 It's reduced. _____ It's at the normal price.

4 It's at the retail price. _____ It's at the wholesale price.

5 It's a big discount. _____ It's a great reduction.

6 It's on sale. _____ It's at the normal retail price.

Exercise 3

Match the words with their definitions.

a) refund	c) exchange	e) receipt	g) credit card
b) credit	d) guarantee	f) check	

1 _____ a piece of paper that says that you bought something in a store

2 _____ money that you get back after you return goods to a store

3 _____ a piece of paper promising you money, a replacement or repair if something goes wrong with what you bought

4 _____ a piece of plastic that you can use like money to pay for goods

5 _____ a piece of paper that says you can spend money in that store

6 _____ goods in return for goods that you bought in a store

7 _____ a piece of paper that says that you will pay with money in your bank

Dictionary work

Each of the words in the box is a type of store. Match the stores with examples of what they sell. Do as many as you can and then check your answers in a dictionary.

a) stationery store	c) jewelry store	e) delicatessen	g) florist's	i) bakery
b) department store	d) hardware store	f) supermarket	h) drugstore	j) liquor store

1 _____ alcoholic drinks

2 _____ sandwiches, salads, soda

3 _____ rings and necklaces

4 _____ bread and cake

5 _____ paper and pens

6 _____ tools

7 _____ medicine

8 _____ flowers

9 _____ milk, fruit, pet food, meat

10 _____ clothes, TVs, perfume

Think about

1 Do most stores in your country give refunds or credits to dissatisfied customers?

2 When are the biggest sales in the stores in your country? Can you get good bargains?

3 Do people usually shop in big department stores and supermarkets, or small shops? Which do you prefer and why?

3.5 Money

Words in context *Read the story and do the exercises.*

Frank García was a young man with very little money, but very big dreams. He worked in a factory and **earned** only $200 a week. He **owned** almost nothing — some old furniture and some clothes, but he dreamed of having a big house and a big car.

Every day Frank **bought** five lottery tickets for one dollar each. He dreamed that one day he would win first prize in the lottery and become a millionaire. Then he could **afford** to buy whatever he wanted and would never have to work another day in his life.

One day as usual Frank opened the newspaper to check his numbers. He read the numbers slowly, "6—11—31—32—47—49." Those were his numbers! He looked again. "6—11—31—32—47—49." He had won. He had won the lottery. He was a millionaire!

Suddenly everyone wanted to be Frank's friend. Many people came to him and asked if they could **borrow** money. "Of course, we'll **pay back** every penny," they said. Others told him about their wonderful ideas for **making money**. "If you **invest** $100,000 in this project," they said, "I promise in two years you will **make a** big **profit** and double your money."

The money had come easily and Frank **spent** it easily. He **lent** $5,000 to this friend and $10,000 to that. He invested $100,000 here and $200,000 there. He made no effort to **save** anything.

When he bought something he never looked at the price. If something **cost** a thousand dollars, he paid a thousand dollars. He never worried about whether it was **worth** it or not. He bought cars, jewelry, and clothes. He also bought airline tickets. He flew first class to all the major cities of the world. He stayed at the best hotels, he ate at the best restaurants, and he bought the finest clothes.

Then one day, when he went to pay his bill at a hotel in Rio, the manager had to tell him, "I'm sorry sir, but I'm afraid your credit card company will not pay this bill."

Frank flew home. It was true he had no more money. He went back to the people who **owed** him money, but they were unable to **repay** him. The projects in which he had invested his money had all **lost money**. In six months Frank had spent $2 million.

Frank now had no choice. He had to sell the cars, the watches and the clothes and he had to go back to work in the factory.

Exercise 1

Find the correct ending for each sentence according to the information in the story.

1 _____ Frank used to earn	a) a lot of money from him.
2 _____ Frank used to buy	b) him a lot of money.
3 _____ Frank used to own	c) $2 million.
4 _____ Frank won	d) money in some of his friend's ideas.
5 _____ Frank's friends borrowed	e) $200 a week.
6 _____ Frank invested	f) the money he had lent them.
7 _____ Frank's friends owed	g) lottery tickets every day.
8 _____ Frank's friends couldn't repay	h) old clothes and some old furniture.

Exercise 2

Decide which phrase correctly finishes each sentence.

1 If I lend you money .
   a) you owe me money.
   b) I owe you money.

2 If I borrow money from you
   a) you should pay me back.
   b) I should repay you.

3 If you can't afford things
   a) you can borrow money from me.
   b) you can lend me money.

4 If I sell something for more than I paid for it
   a) I have lost money.
   b) I have made a profit.

5 If I buy something and pay more than it's worth
   a) I will probably lose money when I sell it.
   b) I will probably make a profit when I sell it.

Exercise 3

Fill each blank with one of the words listed below.

spend	lend	cost	worth	afford
own	earn	sell	invest	save

In the United States and Great Britain, many people would like to _____ their own homes, but it is usually very difficult to _____ enough money. Most people _____ as much as they _____ each month. But if you can't _____ to buy a house, often you can get a bank to _____ you most of the money to buy one. The bank knows that a house is a very good place for you to _____ your money. A few years after you buy it, a house is usually _____ much more than it originally _____ you, so you can _____ it for a big profit.

Dictionary work

Match the words with their definitions. Do as many as you can and then check your answers in the dictionary.

> a) fees b) interest c) taxes d) wages e) salary f) rent g) pension h) fare i) cash j) change

1 _____ money paid for a place to live

2 _____ money paid to the government

3 _____ money paid for professional services

4 _____ money in coins and bills, not checks

5 _____ money paid to workers by the hour or week

6 _____ money paid as charges on the money you borrow

7 _____ money paid to workers for a month's or year's work

8 _____ money paid to older people who no longer work

9 _____ money returned to you after you pay too much

10 _____ money paid for a trip by bus, train or plane

Think about

1 Where does the money go? What percentage of your money do you spend on food, transportation, housing, taxes, clothes and entertainment?

2 One of Shakespeare's characters says, "Neither a borrower, nor a lender be." What does it mean? Do you agree?

3 How easy is it for a poor person to become rich in your country?

Vocabulary review

3 At work (Units 3.1–3.5)

3.1 Jobs
blue-collar
boss
businessman/woman
career
doctor
job
manager
nurse
office worker
profession
retire
sales representative
salesperson
secretary
skilled
teacher
unemployed
unskilled
white-collar

3.2 Farm work
ax
barn
bull
cattle
chop
crops
feed
fertilize
field
gather
harvest
hen
manure
pick
plant
plow
raise
reap
shepherd
soil
spray
store v
tractor
vineyard
water v
wheat

3.3 Tools and their uses
bolt
drill
glue
hammer
knife
ladder
nail
nut
pliers
saw
screw
screwdriver
spade
stick
string
tie
tighten
wire
wrench

3.4 Shopping
bakery
bargain
cheap
check
credit
credit card
deal
delicatessen
department store
discount
drugstore
exchange
expensive
florist's
guarantee
hardware store
jewelry store
liquor store
low price
receipt
reduced
reduction
refund
retail price
sale
    on sale

stationery store
supermarket
wholesale price

3.5 Money
afford
borrow
buy
cash
change
cost
earn
fare
fees
interest
invest
lend
money
    lose money
    make money
owe
own
pay back
pension
profit
    make a profit
rent
repay
salary
save
spend
tax
wages
worth
    be worth

Test yourself 5

■■■

Use the words from the **Vocabulary review** to help you fill in the blanks in these sentences. The number of dashes corresponds to the number of letters in the missing word. More than one answer may be possible, but there is always one best answer.

1 I could never _ _ _ _ _ _ a Cadillac. They're much too expensive.

2 The busiest time of the year on a farm is always _ _ _ _ _ _ _ _ time.

3 Teaching is usually a very poorly paid _ _ _ _ _ _ _ _ _ _ _.

4 Many _ _ _ _ _ _ _ _ _ workers are losing their jobs because robots and computers are doing their work.

5 Some famous _ _ _ _ _ _ _ _ _ _ _ stores are Sears, Bloomingdale's and Macy's.

6 We don't have to work so hard when the _ _ _ _ isn't in the office.

7 I haven't got enough cash on me. Is it all right if I pay by _ _ _ _ _ _?

8 She is a very rich woman. She raises horses and _ _ _ _ _ _ on her ranch in Wyoming.

9 Because I work for a dress shop, I can get a 20 percent _ _ _ _ _ _ _ _ on any clothes I buy.

10 Have you seen the _ _ _ _ _ _ _ _ _ _ _ _? I need it to tighten these screws.

11 George was the best _ _ _ _ _ _ _ _ _ _ _ in the store last year. He sold three thousand pairs of shoes.

12 Be careful while you are cutting the wood. This _ _ _ is very sharp.

13 This year I _ _ _ _ _ _ _ _ some tomatoes in my garden. I hope they grow.

14 I bought this stereo for $200. I think that was a real _ _ _ _ _ _ _ _.

15 In many countries the government takes money in _ _ _ _ _ out of people's pay.

16 Pass me the hammer and some _ _ _ _ _ _, and I'll fix this broken chair.

17 The farmer taught his son how to drive the _ _ _ _ _ _ _ _ across the fields.

18 I haven't got enough money on me. Could you _ _ _ _ _ me some till tomorrow?

19 You can probably fix that broken cup with some good _ _ _ _ _.

20 In some countries, when you're _ _ _ _ _ _ _ _ _ _ _ _, the government will give you money to live on until you find a job.

21 You'll need a longer _ _ _ _ _ _ to reach these windows. They're very high.

22 In which month do the farmers _ _ _ _ _ their grapes in California?

23 If you want to return anything to that store, you'll have to show your _ _ _ _ _ _ _ _.

24 You borrowed $100 from me last year. Now you _ _ _ me $120,

25 because I am charging you 20 percent _ _ _ _ _ _ _ _.

3.6 Education

This is a conversation between Tom, a **senior** in **high school** and an old friend, Mark, who has just started going to Boston **University**.

TOM

MARK

Hi, Mark. How's **school**?

Great. I'm having such a good time. I'm **studying** a lot harder than I did in high school, but it's a lot more fun.

I can't believe you're in **college** already.

Yeah, I know. It seems like yesterday that we were in **elementary school**. Now here I am a **freshman** in college, and next year you will be too.

If I **pass** all my **exams**..

Of course you will. Listen, why don't you relax tonight. Take a night off and come out with me.

I can't. I've got to study for an exam tomorrow.

What exam are you **taking**?

It's one of Davis's history **tests**.

Oh, I remember Davis's history tests. You don't have to worry about them. His tests are always easy. Nobody ever **fails**.

Well, I'm in real trouble if I don't pass.

Listen, you're a good **student**, aren't you?

Yes, but . . .

You went to all his **classes**, right?

Yes, of course, but . . .

And did you **take** good **notes**?

Yes, I took pages and pages of notes in a big notebook and . . .

And did you **do** all the **homework**?

Yes, I kept it all in my notebook with my notes.

And did you write all the **essays** you had to do?

Yes, they're all together in the same big notebook.

So, why are you worried?

There's only one problem. I lost the notebook.

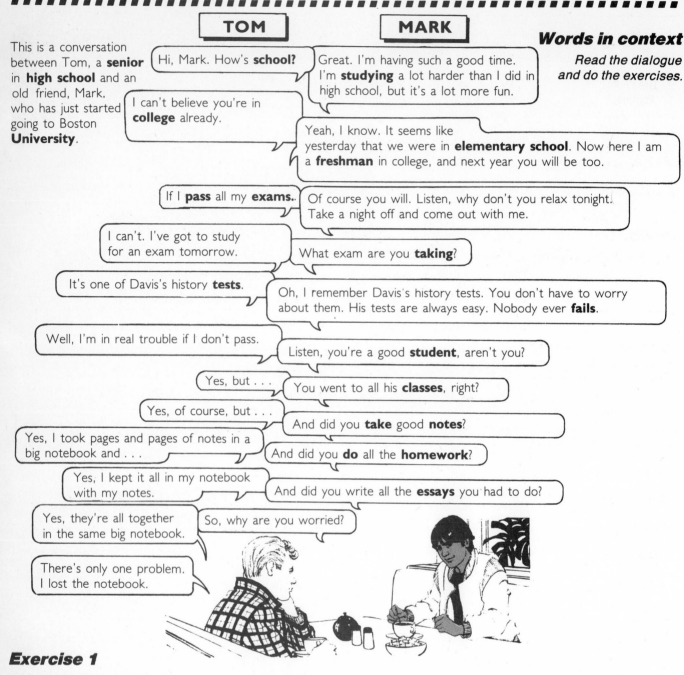

Exercise 1

Choose the best answers according to the information in the dialogue.

1 Who is probably older?
   a) Tom   b) Mark   c) impossible to know

2 How many years have Tom and Mark known each other?
   a) about four b) about twelve c) impossible to know

3 What does Mark think of college compared to high school?
   a) It's easier.   b) It's harder.   c) It's the same.

4 Has Mark ever taken Davis's history test?
   a) yes   b) no   c) impossible to know

5 Is Tom a good student?
   a) yes   b) no   c) impossible to know

6 Is Tom going to fail his history test?
   a) yes   b) no   c) impossible to know

Exercise 2

Put the following words into one of the three columns.

| freshman | essay | homework | college | elementary school | senior | student | notes | university |

place for learning	person who studies	something produced by a student
_____	_____	_____
_____	_____	_____
_____	_____	_____

Exercise 3

Put the following events in order of which happens first, second and third.

1 ____ ____ ____	a) take an exam	b) pass an exam	c) study for an exam
2 ____ ____ ____	a) go to college	b) go to high school	c) go to elementary school
3 ____ ____ ____	a) learn	b) listen	c) forget
4 ____ ____ ____	a) be a teacher	b) be a college freshman	c) be a college senior
5 ____ ____ ____	a) go to class	b) do homework	c) take a test

Just for fun

Which of the following characteristics do you like best in a teacher? Put them in order from 1–8.

is friendly _____

gives frequent tests _____

has a good sense of humor _____

makes a subject interesting _____

gives a lot of homework _____

is young and attractive _____

keeps good control of the students' behavior _____

knows his or her subject well _____

Discuss your answers with someone else.

Think about

1 At what ages do you take important exams in your country?
2 Describe the education system in your country.
3 What subjects do you think are the most important to study at school?
4 Do you think a good education should prepare you for life in general or for a particular job?

3.7 Medical matters

Doctor Lennox is a radio doctor. She answers listeners' questions about their medical problems. Read their questions to her.

Words in context

Read the passages and do the exercises.

a)

Hello, Doctor Lennox. Well, three days ago I fell over and cut my arm. There was a little blood, but it quickly stopped **bleeding** and I forgot about it. Now the **wound** is painful and red. It **hurts** when I touch it. I also think I may have a **fever**. I feel a little hot and quite weak. Do you think I should see my doctor?

b)

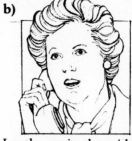

Doctor Lennox, I am a 63-year-old woman. A few months ago, I was walking upstairs when I suddenly felt very **faint** and almost fell over. Now, whenever I do just a little exercise I get **out of breath** very quickly. Even when I'm sleeping, I have breathing problems. I wake up in the middle of the night and can't get back to sleep. I'm really worried, because I have never had **insomnia** in my life before. I don't have a **pain** in my chest, so I don't think I have heart problems. I'm very worried. What do you think?

c)

For the last two days, Doctor Lennox, I have been feeling absolutely terrible. My whole body **aches**. I have a **backache** and all my muscles ache. I have a terrible **headache** too. But the worst thing is the **vomiting**. Food just won't stay in my stomach for more than a few minutes. And the **diarrhea** — I'm in the bathroom every half an hour. I called my doctor and asked for a **prescription** for some medicine, but she said there wasn't much she could do for me. She said I should stay in bed and drink a lot of liquids. Is that right?

d)

I hope you can understand me all right, doctor, but I can't talk very well because of my **sore throat**. I've had it a few months now. And a **cough**, too, even though I don't smoke. And I seem to be tired all the time, but I'm never so sick that I can't go to work. I've been to the doctor and had some tests, but they can't find anything wrong with me. What do you think I should do now?

Exercise 1

Here are Doctor Lennox's answers.
Match her answers to the questions.

1 _____
You should see a doctor as soon as possible. Your doctor will arrange for you to have a complete series of tests. It's best to take care of these things right away.

2 _____
You've probably got a minor infection. Sometimes they take a long time to go away. The important thing is to get plenty of rest. And maybe you should get an opinion from another doctor.

3 _____
It sounds as if you have an infection. You'll have to see your doctor, who will probably write you a prescription for an antibiotic and some medicine to put on your skin as well.

4 _____
You probably have the flu. It's very important that you drink a lot of liquids. You should feel better soon, but if it continues much longer you should see your doctor.

Exercise 2

Complete the first half of each sentence with the best second half.

1 If you have a fever	_____	a) you have some pain and redness.
2 If you feel faint	_____	b) you have difficulty sleeping.
3 If you have insomnia	_____	c) you feel hot.
4 If you have a sore throat	_____	d) your chest may hurt.
5 If you have a bad cough	_____	e) the contents of your stomach come out of your mouth.
6 If you have an infected wound	_____	f) you have difficulty talking and swallowing.
7 If you vomit	_____	g) you have difficulty standing up.

Exercise 3

Read the sentences. Then decide who is most likely to be saying them.

a) "My fingers hurt."	d) "My knees are killing me."
b) "I have a terrible pain in my chest."	e) "I have such a terrible headache."
c) "I've got a bad stomachache	f) "My shoulder is aching terribly."

1 _____ Someone who had to sit for four hours in a plane near a noisy engine.

2 _____ Someone who has just ridden a bike 100 miles.

3 _____ Someone who has eaten some food which was not fresh.

4 _____ Someone who tried to lift something that was too heavy for him.

5 _____ Someone who closed a door on her hand.

6 _____ Someone who is having a heart attack.

Just for fun

If someone told you that they had one of the following medical problems, what would you tell them to do to help them get better quickly?

1 a headache   5 a burn on the finger
2 a sore throat   6 a nosebleed
3 a cough   7 insomnia
4 diarrhea   8 sore muscles after exercise

Discuss your answers with someone else.

Think about

1 Is it expensive to visit the doctor in your country?

2 If you could be a doctor, which type would you be and why?

3 What are the most common symptoms (signs) of flu?

Words in context *Read the newspaper article and answer the questions.*

JURY FINDS MULLINS GUILTY

A **jury** of seven men and five women said today that 78-year-old Mr. Andrew Mullins was **guilty** of murdering his 80-year-old wife, Edith. Six weeks ago, Mullins **went on trial** for murder.

During the trial Mullins said that he had killed his wife because she was very sick and in a lot of pain. He said, "The woman I killed was not my wife. It was a body in pain and a mind with no memory."

He **committed the crime** on the night of August 10th in their home in the small town of Palmston Beach. That morning his wife had looked at him with empty eyes and asked, "Who are you?" That evening she was in terrible pain and kept saying, "Help me, help me." So as she slept on the sofa that night, Mullins put a gun against her head and shot her. Then he called the police and told them what he had done. The police came to the house and **arrested** him. He was later **charged** with murder.

During the six-week trial, there were many **witnesses** who **gave evidence**. The **prosecution** called witnesses who said that Mrs. Mullins liked to go out, that she smiled and wore make-up. The **defense** called doctors who said that Mrs. Mullins was in great pain, and friends who said that Mr. Mullins loved his wife very much. But in the end the jury **reached a verdict** of guilty. They agreed with the prosecutor. It was murder.

Tomorrow the **judge** will **sentence** Mullins. The law says that he must **send** Mullins **to prison** for at least twenty-five years. That means he will not **be released** from prison until he is 103 years old!

There are many people in Palmston Beach tonight who think the law is wrong. Mullins is not a **criminal**. He is not a dangerous man. Perhaps he is just a man who loved his wife too much.

Exercise 1

Ask the questions to the following answers.

1 78. _____

2 Six weeks ago. _____

3 He shot her. _____

4 Acquaintances, doctors and friends.

_____

5 At least twenty-five years.

_____

6 When he is 103 years old.

_____

? Do you think Mullins should go to prison?

Exercise 2

Match the people on the left with what they do during a trial.

1 The judge _____	a)	gives evidence.
2 A witness _____	b)	reaches a verdict of innocent or guilty.
3 The jury _____	c)	tries to show that the person on trial is guilty.
4 The prosecution _____	d)	controls the trial and sentences the guilty person.

Exercise 3

Put the following events in the story of Charles Mercer in the order in which they are most likely to have happened.

1 First, _____	a)	the jury reached a verdict.
2 Later _____	b)	he was arrested by the police.
3 Next, _____	c)	the jury considered the evidence.
4 So then _____	d)	he was sent to prison.
5 And _____	e)	Charles Mercer committed a crime.
6 And _____	f)	the police charged him with the crime.
7 Then _____	g)	he was released from prison.
8 Then _____	h)	the judge sentenced him.
9 After that _____	i)	he went on trial.
10 So _____	j)	the prosecution called witnesses.
11 A few years later _____	k)	the defense said that he was not a criminal.

Dictionary work

Match the names of different crimes to examples of those crimes. Do as many as you can and then check your answers in the dictionary.

a) hijacking	c) burglary	e) kidnapping	g) blackmail
b) shoplifting	d) rape	f) drug-dealing	h) smuggling

1 _____ taking a child away from his or her family

2 _____ not paying taxes on goods from another country

3 _____ getting money by promising not to tell a secret

4 _____ selling cocaine

5 _____ forcing somebody to have sex

6 _____ taking control of an airplane by force

7 _____ taking things from a store without paying

8 _____ going into a house and stealing

Think about

1 What are the most common crimes in your country?

2 Do you think crime has increased in the last twenty-five years? If you do, what do you think are the reasons?

3 What do you think is the best way to fight crime?

3.9 Politics

Words in context

Read the passage
and do the
exercises.

How can you become the leader of a country?

The usual way is to become a **politician** and then to become the leader of the most popular **political party**. In most countries where there are elections to choose the **government**, the **voters** do not usually **elect** their leaders directly. They usually **vote for** a **candidate** who will represent the local region. The candidate who receives the most votes becomes the political representative for that region and takes a seat in the national **parliament** or **assembly**. The political party which wins the most seats has the right to form a government and take power. The head of that political party then becomes the **president** (in countries such as Taiwan or Italy) or the **prime minister** (in countries such as Great Britain and Japan).

In countries such as the United States and France, the system is a little different. Every four years in the United States, and every seven years in France, there are **presidential elections**. At this time the people vote directly for the person that they want to to become president. Regional elections are independent from presidential elections. This means that it is possible to become the President and yet not be the leader of the most popular political party.

There is another more unusual way to become the leader of a country, and that is to be born into the country's **royal family**. If you are a **prince**, especially the eldest son, then one day you can become **king**. And in some countries, if you are the oldest daughter (a **princess**) and there are no sons, then one day you could become **queen**. Of course, today there are not many royal families, and many of those that still exist do not usually have the power to make laws and **govern**.

Exercise 1

Choose the best answer.

1 In most electoral systems, the regional candidate who gets the most votes
   a) does not usually belong to a political party
   b) will represent that region in the national parliament
   c) will form a government and take power

2 In a country such as Great Britain, the political leader
   a) belongs to the royal family
   b) is called the president
   c) belongs to the most popular political party

3 In the United States, the person who becomes President
   a) always belongs to the most popular political party
   b) changes every seven years
   c) is elected directly by the people

4 In a royal family, where there are three sons and two daughters, who is the most likely to become the next king or queen?
   a) the oldest son   b) the oldest daughter
   c) the oldest child

Exercise 2

Match the people on the left with the best definitions on the right.

1 _____ king   a) female relative of a royal family

2 _____ president   b) the head of government in Japan

3 _____ queen   c) someone who chooses a political representative

4 _____ princess   d) male head of a royal family

5 _____ voter   e) female head of a royal family

6 _____ candidate   f) the head of government in the United States

7 _____ prime minister g) male relative of a royal family

8 _____ prince   h) someone who tries to win a place in the national assembly

Exercise 3

Underline the correct word in the following sentences and decide whether the word is a
noun (N), a verb (V) or an adjective (A).

1 _____ Are you interested in (politics/political)?

2 _____ In many countries under 50 percent of the people actually (vote/voter) in an election.

3 _____ The people who (govern/government) the country are called the

4 _____ (govern/government).

5 _____ In France they (elect/election) a new leader every seven years

6 _____ in a (presidential/president)

7 _____ (elect/election).

8 _____ He is the most important (political/politician) in his

9 _____ (political/politician) party.

Dictionary work

Each word in English which has two or more syllables has a strong stress or emphasis
on one of the syllables. Underline the strong-stressed syllable as in the example. Do you know what
the words mean? Do as many as you can and then check the answers in your dictionary.

Example: el<u>ec</u>tion

1 republic	4 president	7 conservative	10 ambassador	13 politics
2 political	5 politician	8 democracy	11 democratic	14 industry
3 industrial	6 society	9 social	12 economy	15 economic

Think about

1 Can you describe how a person becomes the political leader of your country?

2 Which countries have royal families? Do these royal families have much political power?

3 Do you have political parties in your country? What are the differences between them?

3.10 Space

Words in context *Read the passage and do the exercises.*

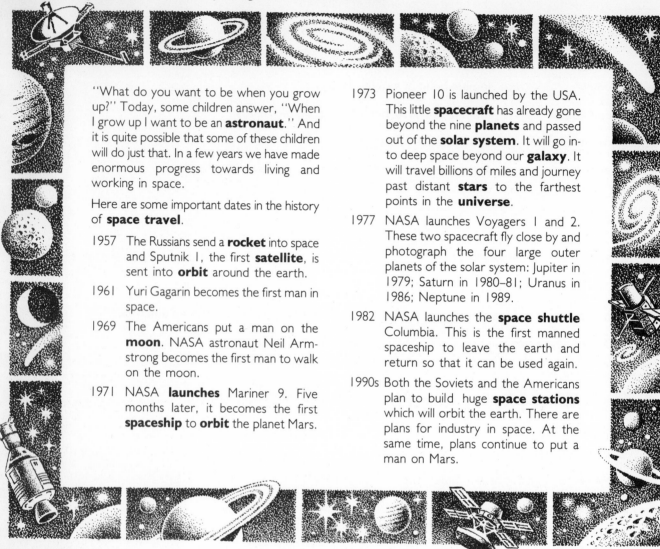

"What do you want to be when you grow up?" Today, some children answer, "When I grow up I want to be an **astronaut**." And it is quite possible that some of these children will do just that. In a few years we have made enormous progress towards living and working in space.

Here are some important dates in the history of **space travel**.

1957 The Russians send a **rocket** into space and Sputnik 1, the first **satellite**, is sent into **orbit** around the earth.

1961 Yuri Gagarin becomes the first man in space.

1969 The Americans put a man on the **moon**. NASA astronaut Neil Armstrong becomes the first man to walk on the moon.

1971 NASA **launches** Mariner 9. Five months later, it becomes the first **spaceship** to **orbit** the planet Mars.

1973 Pioneer 10 is launched by the USA. This little **spacecraft** has already gone beyond the nine **planets** and passed out of the **solar system**. It will go into deep space beyond our **galaxy**. It will travel billions of miles and journey past distant **stars** to the farthest points in the **universe**.

1977 NASA launches Voyagers 1 and 2. These two spacecraft fly close by and photograph the four large outer planets of the solar system: Jupiter in 1979; Saturn in 1980–81; Uranus in 1986; Neptune in 1989.

1982 NASA launches the **space shuttle** Columbia. This is the first manned spaceship to leave the earth and return so that it can be used again.

1990s Both the Soviets and the Americans plan to build huge **space stations** which will orbit the earth. There are plans for industry in space. At the same time, plans continue to put a man on Mars.

Exercise 1

Decide if the following statements are true (T) or false (F) according to the information in the passage.

1 _____ The Russians sent a man into space in 1957.

2 _____ American astronauts landed on the moon in 1969.

3 _____ Mariner 9 landed on Mars in 1971.

4 _____ It took nine years for Voyager 2 to reach Uranus.

5 _____ Pioneer 10 is still traveling in space.

6 _____ A space shuttle has been orbiting the earth since 1982.

7 _____ In the 1990s there are plans to put a space station into orbit around Mars.

Exercise 2

Fill in the blank with the correct missing word or words, so that each pair of items in column B has the same relationship as each pair in column A.

	A		**B**
1	pilot : plane	_____	: spaceship
2	take off : plane	_____	: rocket
3	flight path : plane	_____	: satellite

Exercise 3

Put the following into order from smallest (1) to largest (7).

a) galaxy	b) universe	c) planet	d) moon	e) solar system	f) star	g) space shuttle

1 ____ 2 ____ 3 ____ 4 ____ 5 ____ 6 ____ 7 ____ 8 ____

Just for fun

Do you know the position of the planets in our solar system? See if you can name the planets on the diagram below.

a) Earth	b) Jupiter	c) Venus	d) Saturn	e) Mercury	f) Mars	g) Uranus	h) Pluto	i) Neptune

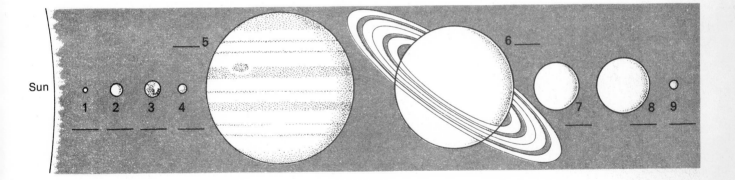

Think about

1 Do you think space exploration is important?

2 Has your country been involved in space exploration in any way?

3 Do you think that in the future many people will travel to other planets and live in spaceships? Would you like to?

4 Is there life on other planets?

Vocabulary review

3 At work (Units 3.6–3.10)

3.6 Education
class
college
elementary school
essay
exam
fail a test/an exam
freshman
high school
homework
  do homework
lecture
notes
  take notes
pass a test/an exam
senior
student
study
take a test/an exam
test
university

3.7 Medical matters
ache
backache
bleed
cough
diarrhea
faint
fever
  have a fever
headache
hurt
insomnia
out of breath
pain
prescription
throat
  sore throat
vomit
wound

3.8 The law
arrest
blackmail
burglary
charge *v*
crime
  commit a crime
criminal
defense
drug-dealing
evidence
  give evidence
go on trial
guilty
hijacking
judge
jury
kidnapping
police
prison
prosecutor
rape
release from prison
send to prison
sentence *v*
shoplifting
smuggling
trial
verdict
  reach a verdict
witness

3.9 Politics
ambassador
assembly
candidate
conservative
democracy
democratic
economic
economy
elect
election
govern

government
industrial
industry
king
parliament
political
political party
politician
politics
president
presidential
prime minister
prince
princess
queen
republic
royal family
social
society
vote
voter

3.10 Space
astronaut
galaxy
launch
moon
orbit
planet
rocket
satellite
send into orbit
solar system
spacecraft
space shuttle
space station
space travel
star
universe

Test yourself 6

Use the words from the **Vocabulary review** to help you fill in the blanks in these sentences. The number of dashes corresponds to the number of letters in the missing word have been given to help you. More than one answer may be possible, but there is always one best answer.

1 Before the Americans sent an _ _ _ _ _ _ _ _ _ into space, they sent a dog.

2 The exam seemed very difficult. I think I must have _ _ _ _ _ _.

3 In the last presidential election, what percentage of the population _ _ _ _ _?

4 Which is the nearest _ _ _ _ _ _ to the Earth?

5 Would you go to work if you had a _ _ _ _ _ of 100°F?

6 Whenever I sit in the smoking section of an airplane, I get a terrible _ _ _ _ _ _ _ _ _.

7 The judge sentenced the two men to twenty years in _ _ _ _ _ _ _.

8 They were found guilty of _ _ _ _ _ _ _ _ _ _. They had taken the young son of a rich businessman and demanded $20 million.

9 In 1986 the space _ _ _ _ _ _ _ Challenger exploded after take-off, killing all seven astronauts.

10 The professor asked the students what they were going to do when they finished _ _ _ _ _ _ _.

11 There is one side of the _ _ _ _ which can never be seen from the Earth.

12 There is a great deal of international interest in the British royal family, especially in the princes and _ _ _ _ _ _ _ _ _.

13 When the teacher asked for last night's _ _ _ _ _ _ _ _, Miriam said she hadn't done it.

14 People who smoke often have a bad _ _ _ _ _.

15 There were six people who said they had seen the crime, but each _ _ _ _ _ _ _ said they had seen something different.

16 A political system where the people vote for the government is usually called a _ _ _ _ _ _ _ _ _.

17 The political and _ _ _ _ _ _ _ _ systems of the United States and the Soviet Union are very different.

18 One of the first signs of a heart attack is a sharp _ _ _ _ in the left arm.

19 Most college _ _ _ _ _ _ _ _ find their first year at school difficult.

20 After I have my teeth cleaned at the dentist's, they _ _ _ _ for a day or two.

21 The police _ _ _ _ _ _ _ _ him after finding his fingerprints on the gun.

22 There are a great many telecommunications _ _ _ _ _ _ _ _ _ _ orbiting the Earth.

23 At what age do you have to _ _ _ _ important exams in your country.

24 In Japan the head of the _ _ _ _ _ _ _ _ _ _ is called the Prime Minister.

25 The jury listened to a great deal of evidence during a very long _ _ _ _ _ _.

Index

accuse/ə'kyuʷz/ 2.10
ache/eʸk/ 3.7
actor/'æktər/ 2.6
actress/'æktrɪs/ 2.6
advertisement 2.8
/ˌædvər'taɪzmənt/
advise/əd'vaɪz/ 2.10
afford/ə'fɔrd/ 3.5
aftershave/'æftər ˌʃeʸv/ 1.4
agree/ə'griʸ/ 2.10
ambassador/æm'bæsədər/ 3.9
amusing/ə'myuʷzɪŋ/ 2.5
apologize/ə'palə ˌdzaɪz/ 2.10
appendix/ə'pɛndɪks/ 2.9
argument/'argyəmənt/ 2.10
armchair/'armtʃɛər/ 1.2
arrest/ə'rɛst/ 3.8
art gallery/'art ˌgæləriʸ/ 2.4
article/'arṭɪkəl/ 2.9
ashtray/'æʃtreʸ/ 1.2
asleep/ə'sliʸp/ 1.3
assembly/ə'sɛmbliʸ/ 3.9
astronaut/'æstrə ˌnɔt/ 3.10
atlas/'ætləs/ 2.9
avocado/ˌævə'kadoʷ/ 1.6
awake/ə'weʸk/ 1.3
ax/æks/ 3.2

backache/'bækeʸk/ 3.7
backyard/ˌbæk'yard/ 1.1
bad/bæd/ 1.8
bag/bæg/ 1.8
baggy/'bægiʸ/ 1.10
bake/beʸk/ 1.6
bakery/'beʸkəriʸ/ 3.4
ballerina/ˌbælə'riʸnə/ 2.4
ballet/bæ'leʸ/ 2.4
band/bænd/ 2.7
bargain/'bargɪn/ 3.4
barn/barn/ 3.2
bar of soap/ˌbar əv 'soʷp/ 1.4
baseball/'beʸsbɔl/ 2.1
basement/'beʸsmənt/ 1.1
basketball/'bæskɪtˌbɔl/ 2.1
bat/bæt/ 2.2
bath/bæθ/ 1.4
bathtub/'bæθtʌb/ 1.4
bathroom/'bæθruʷm/ 1.1
bean/biʸn/ 1.6
beat/biʸt/ 1.6, 2.7
bed/bɛd/ 1.3, 1.5
bedroom/'bɛdruʷm/ 1.1
beef/biʸf/ 1.6
beg/bɛg/ 2.10
be kidding/biʸ 'kɪdɪŋ/ 2.5
belted/'bɛltɪd/ 1.10
bench/bɛntʃ/ 1.2
be worth/biʸ 'wɜrθ/ 3.5
bibliography/ 2.9
ˌbɪbliʸ'agrəfiʸ/
biography/baɪ'agrəfiʸ/ 2.9
blackmail/'blækmeʸl/ 3.8
blanket/'blæŋkɪt/ 1.3
bleed/bliʸd/ 3.7

blouse/blaʊs/ 1.9
blue-collar/ˌbluʷ 'kalər/ 3.1
boil/bɔɪl/ 1.6
bolt/boʷlt/ 3.3
book/bʊk/ 2.9
bookcase/'bʊk-keʸs/ 1.2
boot/buʷt/ 1.9
boring/'bɔrɪŋ/ 2.3
borrow/'baroʷ/ 3.5
boss/bɔs/ 3.1
bottle/'baṭl/ 1.8
bottled/'baṭld/ 1.8
bowl/boʷl/ 1.7, 1.8
box/baks/ 1.8
boxing/'baksɪŋ/ 2.1
breath/brɛθ/ 3.7
broom/bruʷm/ 1.5
brush your teeth/ˌbrʌʃ yər 1.4
'tiʸθ/
bull/bʊl/ 3.2
burglary/'bɜrgləriʸ/ 3.8
businessman/woman 3.1
/'bɪznɪsˌmæn,-,wʊmən/
button-down/'bʌtn ˌdaʊn/ 1.10
buy/baɪ/ 3.5

cabbage/'kæbɪdʒ/ 1.6
cabinet/'kæbənɪt/ 1.2
cage/keʸdʒ/ 2.4
can/kæn/ 1.8
candidate/'kændəˌdeʸt/ 3.9
canned/kænd/ 1.8
canning/'kænɪŋ/ 1.8
career/kə'rɪər/ 3.1
carpet/'karpɪt/ 1.2
carton/'kartn/ 1.8
cartoon/kar'tuʷn/ 2.8, 2.9
cash/kæʃ/ 3.5
cassette player/kə'sɛt 1.2
ˌpleʸər/
catch/kætʃ/ 2.2
cattle/'kæṭl/ 3.2
CD/ˌsiʸ 'diʸ/ 1.2
ceiling/'siʸlɪŋ/ 1.1
celebrate/'sɛləˌbreʸt/ 2.3
celery/'sɛləriʸ/ 1.6
chair/tʃɛər/ 1.2
change/tʃeʸndʒ/ 3.5
channel/'tʃænl/ 2.8
chapter/'tʃæptər/ 2.9
charge/tʃardʒ/ 3.8
chat/tʃæt/ 2.10
cheap/tʃiʸp/ 3.4
check/tʃɛk/ 3.4
checked/tʃɛkt/ 1.10
chest of drawers/'tʃɛst əv 1.2
'drɔrz/
chew/tʃu/ 1.7
chimney/'tʃɪmniʸ/ 1.1
chop n/tʃap/ 1.6
chop v/tʃap/ 3.2
circus/'sɜrkəs/ 2.4
class/klæs/ 3.6
classical/'klæsɪkəl/ 2.7

classified ad/ˌklæsəˌfaɪd 2.9
'æd/
clean/kliʸn/ 1.5
closet/'klazɪt/ 1.2
cloth/klɔθ/ 1.5
clown/klaʊn/ 2.4, 2.6
club/klʌb/ 2.3
coffee cup/'kɔfiʸ ˌkʌp/ 1.7
coffee table/'kɔfiʸ ˌteʸbəl/ 1.2
college/'kalɪdʒ/ 3.6
column/'kaləm/ 2.9
comedian/kə'miʸdiʸən/ 2.6
comedy/'kamədiʸ/ 2.8
commercial/kə'mɜrʃəl/ 2.8
commit a crime/kə'mɪt ə 3.8
'kraɪm/
commit a foul/kə'mɪt ə 2.2
'faʊl/
compact disc player/ 1.2
ˌkampækt 'dɪsk ˌpleʸər/
computer/kəm'pyuʷṭər/ 1.2
concert/'kansərt/ 2.4
confess/kən'fɛs/ 2.10
consciousness/'kanʃəsnɪs/ 1.3
conservative/kən'sɜrvəṭɪv/ 1.10, 3.9
conversation 2.10
/ˌkanvər'seʸʃən/
cost/kɔst/ 3.5
cough/kɔf/ 3.7
course/kɔrs/ 2.2
crash (a party)/kræʃ/ 2.3
credit/'krɛdɪt/ 3.4
credit card/'krɛdɪt ˌkard/ 3.4
crime/kraɪm/ 3.8
criminal/'krɪmənəl/ 3.8
crops/kraps/ 3.2
crossword puzzle 2.9
/'krɔswɜrd ˌpʌzəl/
cucumber/'kyuʷkʌmbər/ 1.6
cup/kʌp/ 1.7, 1.8
current affairs/ˌkɜrənt 2.8
ə'fɛərz/
curtain/'kɜrtn/ 1.2
cushion/'kʊʃən/ 1.2
cut/kʌt/ 1.7
cycling/'saɪklɪŋ/ 2.1

deal/diʸl/ 3.4
deckchair/'dɛktʃɛər/ 1.2
deep sleep/ˌdiʸp 'sliʸp/ 1.3
defense/dɪ'fɛns/ 3.8
delicatessen/ˌdɛlɪkə'tɛsən/ 3.4
delicious/dɪ'lɪʃəs/ 1.8
democracy/dɪ'makrəsiʸ/ 3.9
democratic/ˌdɛmə'krætɪk/ 3.9
deny/dɪ'naɪ/ 2.10
deodorant/diʸ'oʷdərənt/ 1.4
department store 3.4
/dɪpartmənt stɔr/
desk/dɛsk/ 1.2
detective series/dɪ'tɛktiv 2.8
ˌsɪəriʸz/
diarrhea/ˌdaɪə'riʸə/ 3.7
dictionary/'dɪkʃəˌnɛriʸ/ 2.9

dining room/ˈdaɪnɪŋ ˌruʷm/ 1.1
dining table/ˈdaɪnɪŋ ˌteʸbəl/ 1.2
dinner/ˈdɪnər/ 2.4
dirty/ˈdɜrtiʸ/ 1.5
discount/ˈdɪskaʊnt/ 3.4
discuss/dɪˈskʌs/ 2.10
dishwasher/ˈdɪʃˌwaʃər/ 1.5
disk jockey/ˈdɪsk ˌdʒakiʸ/ 2.4
dive/daɪv/ 2.2
doctor/ˈdaktər/ 3.1
documentary/ˌdakyəˈmɛntariʸ/ 2.8
do homework/duʷ ˈhoʷmwɜrk/ 3.6
do the dishes/duʷ ðə ˈdɪʃəs/ 1.5
downstairs/ˌdaʊnˈstɛərz/ 1.1
drawer/drɔr/ 1.2
dream n/driʸm/ 1.3
dress/drɛs/ 1.9
dried/draɪd/ 1.8
drill/drɪl/ 3.3
drink/drɪŋk/ 1.7
driveway/ˈdraɪvweʸ/ 1.1
drowsy/ˈdraʊziʸ/ 1.3
drug-dealing/ˈdrʌg ˌdiʸlɪŋ/ 3.8
drugstore/ˈdrʌgstɔr/ 3.4
drums/drʌmz/ 2.7
dry yourself/ˈdraɪ yərsɛlf/ 1.4
dust/dʌst/ 1.5

earn/ɜrn/ 3.5
eat/iʸt/ 1.7
economic/ˌɛkəˈnamɪk/ 3.9
economy/ɪˈkanəmiʸ/ 3.9
editorial/ˌɛdəˈtɔriʸəl/ 2.9
elect/ɪˈlɛkt/ 3.9
election/ɪˈlɛkʃən/ 3.9
elementary school /ɛləˈmɛntariʸ ˌskuʷl/ 3.6
encyclopedia /ɪnˌsaɪkləˈpiʸdiʸə/ 2.9
enjoy yourself/ɪnˈdʒɔɪ yərsɛlf/ 2.3
entertainer/ˌɛntərˈteʸnər/ 2.6
essay/ˈɛseʸ/ 3.6
evidence/ˈɛvədəns/ 3.8
exaggerate/ɪgˈzædʒəˌreʸt/ 2.10
exam/ɪgˈzæm/ 3.6
exchange/ɪksˈtʃeʸndʒ/ 3.4
exciting/ɪkˈsaɪtɪŋ/ 2.3
exhausted/ɪgˈzɔstɪd/ 1.3
exhibit/ɪgˈzɪbɪt/ 2.4
expensive/ɪkˈspɛnsɪv/ 3.4

fail (a test/an exam)/feʸl/ 3.6
faint/feʸnt/ 3.7
fall asleep/ˌfɔl əˈsliʸp/ 1.3
fare/fɛər/ 3.5
fashionable/ˈfæʃənəbəl/ 1.10
faucet/ˈfɔsɪt/ 1.4
feed/fiʸd/ 3.2
fees/fiʸz/ 3.5
fence/fɛns/ 1.1
fertilize/ˈfɜrtḷˌaɪz/ 3.2
fever/ˈfiʸvər/ 3.7

fiction/ˈfɪkʃən/ 2.9
field/fiʸld/ 3.2
field hockey/ˈfiʸld ˌhakiʸ/ 2.1
filthy/ˈfɪlθiʸ/ 1.5
fireplace/ˈfaɪərpleʸs/ 1.1
florist's/ˈflɔrɪsts/ 3.4
floor/flɔr/ 1.1
flowered/ˈflaʊərd/ 1.10
flute/fluʷt/ 2.7
folk/foʷk/ 2.7
football/ˈfʊtbɔl/ 2.1
forgive/fərˈgɪv/ 2.10
fork/fɔrk/ 1.7
foul/faʊl/ 2.2
fresh/frɛʃ/ 1.8
freshman/ˈfrɛʃmən/ 3.6
front door/ˌfrʌnt ˈdɔr/ 1.1
front yard/ˌfrʌnt ˈyard/ 1.1
frozen/ˈfroʷzən/ 1.8
fry/fraɪ/ 1.6
frying pan/ˈfraɪ-ɪŋ ˌpæn/ 1.6
fun/fʌn/ 2.3, 2.5
funny/ˈfʌniʸ/ 2.5
furnace/ˈfɜrnɪs/ 1.1

galaxy/ˈgæləksiʸ/ 3.10
game show/ˈgeʸm ˌʃoʷ/ 2.8
garage/gəˈraʒ/ 1.1
garden/ˈgardn/ 1.1
gate/geʸt/ 1.1
gather/ˈgæðər/ 3.2
get up/ˌgɛṭ ˈʌp/ 1.3
gift/gɪft/ 2.3
give a gift/a present/ˌgɪv ə ˈgɪft, ə ˈprɛzənt/ 2.3
give a lecture/ˌgɪv ə ˈlɛktʃər/ 2.10
give a party/ˌgɪv ə ˈparṭiʸ/ 2.3
give a speech/ˌgɪv ə ˈspiʸtʃ/ 2.10
give evidence/ˌgɪv ˈɛvədəns/ 3.8
glass/glæs/ 1.7, 1.8
glossary/ˈglasəriʸ/ 2.9
glove/glʌv/ 1.9
glue/gluʷ/ 3.3
go bad/goʷ ˈbæd/ 1.8
golf/galf/ 2.1
go on trial/ˌgoʷ an ˈtraɪəl/ 3.8
go out to dinner/ˌgoʷ aʊt tə ˈdɪnər/ 2.4
gossip/ˈgasəp/ 2.10
go stale/goʷ ˈsteʸl/ 1.8
go to bed/goʷ tə ˈbɛd/ 1.3
govern/ˈgʌvərn/ 3.9
government/ˈgʌvərmənt/ 3.9
go wild/goʷ ˈwaɪld/ 2.3
grape/greʸp/ 1.6
grate/greʸt/ 1.6
group/gruʷp/ 2.7
guarantee/ˌgærənˈtiʸ/ 3.4
guilty/ˈgɪltiʸ/ 3.8
guitar/gɪˈtar/ 2.7
gymnastics/dʒɪmˈnæstɪks/ 2.1

hall/hɔl/ 1.1
ham/hæm/ 1.6

hammer/ˈhæmər/ 3.3
handball/ˈhændˌbɔl/ 2.1
hardware store/ˈhardwɛər stɔr/ 3.4
harvest/ˈharvɪst/ 3.2
hat/hæt/ 1.9
have a fever/ˌhæv ə ˈfiʸvər/ 3.7
have a good time/ˌhæv ə gʊd ˈtaɪm/ 2.3
have fun/ˌhæv ˈfʌn/ 2.3
headache/ˈhɛdeʸk/ 3.7
headline/ˈhɛdlaɪn/ 2.9
heat/hiʸt/ 1.6
hedge/hɛdʒ/ 1.1
hen/hɛn/ 3.2
high-heeled/ˌhaɪ ˈhiʸld/ 1.10
high school/ˈhaɪ skuʷl/ 3.6
hijacking/ˈhaɪdʒækɪŋ/ 3.8
hit/hɪt/ 2.2
horseback riding/ˈhɔrsbæk ˌraɪdɪŋ/ 2.1
humorous/ˈhyuʷmərəs/ 2.5
hurt/hɜrt/ 3.7

in adj/ɪn/ 1.10
industrial/ɪnˈdʌstriʸəl/ 3.9
industry/ˈɪndəstriʸ/ 3.9
insomnia/ɪnˈsamniʸə/ 3.7
in style/ɪn ˈstaɪl/ 1.10
interest/ˈɪntrɪst/ 3.5
introduction/ˌɪntrəˈdʌkʃən/ 2.9
invest/ɪnˈvɛst/ 3.5
invite/ɪnˈvaɪt/ 2.3
iron/ˈaɪərn/ 1.5

jacket/ˈdʒækɪt/ 1.9
jar/dʒar/ 1.8
jazz/dʒæz/ 2.7
jeans/dʒiʸnz/ 1.9
jewelry store/ˈdʒuʷəlriʸ stɔr/ 3.4
job/dʒab/ 3.1
joke/dʒoʷk/ 2.5
judge/dʒʌdʒ/ 3.8
judo/ˈdʒudoʷ/ 2.1
jump/dʒʌmp/ 2.2
jury/ˈdʒʊəriʸ/ 3.8

kettle/ˈkɛtḷ/ 1.8
kick/kɪk/ 2.2
kid/kɪd/ 2.5
kidding, be/ˈkɪdɪŋ/ 2.5
kidnapping/ˈkɪdnæpɪŋ/ 3.8
king/kɪŋ/ 3.9
kitchen/ˈkɪtʃən/ 1.1
knife/naɪf/ 1.6, 1.7, 3.3

ladder/ˈlædər/ 3.3
lamb/læm/ 1.6
lamp/læmp/ 1.2
launch/lɔntʃ/ 3.10
lecture/ˈlɛktʃər/ 2.10
lend/lɛnd/ 3.5
lick/lɪk/ 1.7
linoleum/lɪˈnoʷliʸəm/ 1.2
lipstick/ˈlɪpˌstɪk/ 1.4
liquor store/ˈlɪkər stɔr/ 3.4

living room/'lɪvɪŋ ˌruʷm/ 1.1
lose money/ˌluʷz 'mʌniʸ/ 3.5
low price/ˌloʷ 'praɪs/ 3.4

magazine/ˌmægə'ziʸn/ 2.9
magician/mə'dʒɪʃən/ 2.6
make a profit/ˌmeʸk ə 'prafɪt/ 3.5
make a pun/ˌmeʸk ə 'pʌn/ 2.5
make fun of/ˌmeʸk 'fʌn əv/ 2.5
make money/ˌmeʸk 'mʌniʸ/ 3.5
make the bed/ˌmeʸk ðə 'bɛd/ 1.5
make-up/'meʸk ʌp/ 1.4
manager/'mænɪdʒər/ 3.1
manure/mə'nʊər/ 3.2
mat/mæt/ 1.2
match/mætʃ/ 2.2
mattress/'mætrɪs/ 1.3
melody/'mɛlədiʸ/ 2.7
melt/mɛlt/ 1.6
mess/mɛs/ 1.5
messy/'mɛsiʸ/ 1.5
mix/mɪks/ 1.6
modern/'madərn/ 1.10
money/'mʌniʸ/ 3.5
moon/muʷn/ 3.10
mop/map/ 1.5
movie/'muʷviʸ/ 2.8
movie director/'muʷviʸ dəˌrɛktər/ 2.6
movies/'muʷviʸz/ 2.4
movie star/'muʷviʸ ˌstar/ 2.6
mug/mʌg/ 1.7, 1.8
mumble/'mʌmbəl/ 2.10
museum/myuʷ'ziʸəm/ 2.4
musician/myuʷ'zɪʃən/ 2.6

nail/neʸl/ 3.3
nail polish/'neʸl ˌpalɪʃ/ 1.4
napkin/'næpkɪn/ 1.7
neat/niʸt/ 1.5
news/nuʷz/ 2.8
newspaper/'nuʷzˌpeʸpər/ 2.9
nightmare/'naɪtmɛər/ 1.3
non-fiction/ˌnan 'fɪkʃən/ 2.9
notes/noʷts/ 3.6
novel/'navəl/ 2.9
nurse/nɜrs/ 3.1
nut/nʌt/ 3.3

office worker/'ɔfɪs ˌwɜrkər/ 3.1
old-fashioned/ˌoʷld 'fæʃənd/ 1.10
on sale/ˌan 'seʸl/ 3.4
opera/'apərə/ 2.4
orbit/'ɔrbɪt/ 3.10
orchestra/'ɔrkɪstrə/ 2.4
organ/'ɔrgən/ 2.7
out-dated/ˌaʊt 'deʸṭɪd/ 1.10
out of breath/ˌaʊt əv 'brɛθ/ 3.7
out of style/ˌaʊt əv 'staɪl/ 1.10
out of work/ˌaʊt əv 'wɜrk/ 3.1
oven/'ʌvən/ 1.6
overcoat/'oʷvərˌkoʷt/ 1.9

owe/oʷ/ 3.5
own/oʷn/ 3.5

package/'pækɪdʒ/ 1.8
pain/peʸn/ 3.7
pajamas/pə'dʒaməz/ 1.3
pants/pænts/ 1.9
paperback/'peʸpərˌbæk/ 2.9
parliament/'parləmənt/ 3.9
party/'partiʸ/ 2.3, 3.9
pass (a ball)/pæs/ 2.2
pass (a test/an exam)/pæs/ 3.6
pay back/peʸ 'bæk/ 3.5
pea/piʸ/ 1.6
peach/piʸtʃ/ 1.6
pear/pɛər/ 1.6
peel/piʸl/ 1.6
pension/'pɛnʃən/ 3.5
perfume/pər'fyuʷm/ 1.4
piano/piʸ'ænoʷ/ 2.7
pick/pɪk/ 3.2
pillow/'pɪloʷ/ 1.3
pineapple/'paɪnˌæpəl/ 1.6
planet/'plænɪt/ 3.10
plant/plænt/ 3.2
plate/pleʸt/ 1.7
play/pleʸ/ 2.9
play a joke on/pleʸ ə 'dʒoʷk an/ 2.5
pleated/'pliʸṭɪd/ 1.10
pliers/'plaɪərz/ 3.3
plow/plaʊ/ 3.2
plum/plʌm/ 1.6
poem/'poʷəm/ 2.9
polish/'palɪʃ/ 1.5
political/pə'lɪṭɪkəl/ 3.9
political party/pəˌlɪṭɪkəl 'partiʸ/ 3.9
politician/ˌpalə'tɪʃən/ 3.9
politics/'paləˌtɪks/ 3.9
popular/'papyələr/ 1.10
pour/pɔr/ 1.6
president/'prɛzədənt/ 3.9
presidential/ˌprɛzə'dɛnʃəl/ 3.9
price/praɪs/ 3.4
prime minister/ˌpraɪm 'mɪnəstər/ 3.9
prince/prɪns/ 3.9
princess/'prɪnsɪs/ 3.9
prison/'prɪzən/ 3.8
profession/prə'fɛʃən/ 3.1
profit/'prafɪt/ 3.5
program/'proʷgræm/ 2.8
promise/ˌpramɪs/ 2.10
prosecution /ˌprasə'kyuʷʃən/ 3.8
pull someone's leg/ˌpʊl sʌmwʌnz 'lɛg/ 2.5
pun/pʌn/ 2.5
punk rock/pʌŋk rak/ 2.7

queen/kwiʸn/ 3.9

radio/'reʸdiʸˌoʷ/ 1.2
raise v/reʸz/ 3.2
rape/reʸp/ 3.8
raw/rɔ/ 1.8

reach a verdict/ˌriʸtʃ ə 'vɜrdɪkt/ 3.8
reap/riʸp/ 3.2
receipt/rɪ'siʸt/ 3.4
record n/'rɛkərd/ 1.2
reduced/rɪ'duʷst/ 3.4
reduction/rɪ'dʌkʃən/ 3.4
referee/ˌrɛfə'riʸ/ 2.2
refund n/'riʸfʌnd/ 3.4
reggae/'rɛgeʸ/ 2.7
release from prison/rɪˌliʸs frəm prɪ'zən/ 3.8
rent/rɛnt/ 3.5
repay/rɪ'peʸ/ 3.5
republic/rɪ'pʌblɪk/ 3.9
retail price/'riʸteʸl praɪs/ 3.4
rhythm/'rɪðəm/ 2.7
riddle/'rɪdl/ 2.5
rock/rak/ 2.7
rock club/'rak clʌb/ 2.3
rocket/'rakɪt/ 3.10
rock 'n' roll/ˌrak ən 'roʷl/ 2.7
rock star/'rak star/ 2.6
roof/ruʷf/ 1.1
rot/rat/ 1.8
rotten/'ratn/ 1.8
rowing/'roʷɪŋ/ 2.1
royal family/ˌrɔɪəl 'fæməliʸ/ 3.9
rug/rʌg/ 1.2
rugby/'rʌgbiʸ/ 2.1
run/rʌn/ 2.2

sailing/'seʸlɪŋ/ 2.1
salary/'sæləriʸ/ 3.5
sale/seʸl/ 3.4
salesperson/'seʸlzˌpərsən/ 3.1
sales representative/'seʸlz rɛprɪˌzɛntəṭɪv/ 3.1
salted/'sɔltɪd/ 1.8
satellite/'sæṭlˌaɪt/ 3.10
saucepan/'sɔs-pæn/ 1.6
saucer/'sɔsər/ 1.7
sausage/'sɔsɪdʒ/ 1.6
save/seʸv/ 3.5
saw/sɔ/ 3.3
saxophone/'sæksəˌfoʷn/ 2.7
scarf/skarf/ 1.9
score/skɔr/ 2.2
screen/skriʸn/ 2.4
screw/skruʷ/ 3.3
screwdriver/ 'skruʷˌdraɪvər/ 3.3
scrub/skrʌb/ 1.5
scrub brush/'skrʌb brʌʃ/ 1.5
secretary/'sɛkrəˌtɛriʸ/ 3.1
see the sights/siʸ ðə 'saɪts/ 2.4
send into orbit/ˌsɛnd ɪntə 'ɔrbɪt/ 3.10
send to prison/ˌsɛnd tə 'prɪzən/ 3.8
senior/'siʸnyər/ 3.6
sentence v/'sɛntəns/ 3.8
series/'sɪəriʸz/ 2.7
serve/sɜrv/ 2.2
set n/sɛt/ 2.2
shampoo/ʃæm'puʷ/ 1.4

shaving cream/'ʃeʸvɪŋ kriʸm/ 1.4

sheet/ʃiʸt/ 1.3

shelf/ʃɛlf/ 1.2

shepherd/'ʃɛpərd/ 3.2

shine/ʃaɪn/ 1.5

shirt/ʃɜrt/ 1.9

shoe/ʃuʷ/ 1.9

shoot/ʃuʷt/ 2.2

shooting/'ʃuʷtɪŋ/ 2.1

shoplifting/'ʃap,lɪftɪŋ/ 3.8

shorts/ʃɔrts/ 1.9

short-sleeved/,ʃɔrt 'sliʸvd/ 1.10

shout/ʃaʊt/ 2.10

show n/ʃoʷ/ 2.8

shower/'ʃaʊər/ 1.4

sights/saɪts/ 2.4

sightseeing/'saɪt,siʸɪŋ/ 2.4

silly/'sɪliʸ/ 2.5

singer/'sɪŋər/ 2.6

sink n/sɪŋk/ 1.4

skilled/skɪld/ 3.1

skirt/skɜrt/ 1.9

sleepy/'sliʸpiʸ/ 1.3

slice/slaɪs/ 1.6

smoked/smoʷkt/ 1.8

smuggling/'smʌglɪŋ/ 3.8

soap opera/'soʷp ,apərə/ 2.8

soccer/'sakər/ 2.1

social/'soʷʃəl/ 3.9

society/sə'saɪətiʸ/ 3.9

sock/sak/ 1.9

sofa/'soʷfə/ 1.2

soil/sɔɪl/ 3.2

solar system/'soʷlər ,sɪstəm/ 3.10

sore throat/sɔr 'θroʷt/ 3.7

sour/saʊər/ 1.8

spacecraft/'speʸs-kræft/ 3.10

spaceship/'speʸs,ʃɪp/ 3.10

space shuttle/'speʸs ,ʃʌtl/ 3.10

space station/'speʸs ,steʸʃən/ 3.10

space travel/'speʸs ,trævəl/ 3.10

spade/speʸd/ 3.3

speech/spiʸtʃ/ 2.10

spend/spɛnd/ 3.5

spinach/'spɪnɪtʃ/ 1.6

spoon/spuʷn/ 1.6, 1.7

sports show/'spɔrts ʃoʷ/ 2.8

spotless/'spatlɪs/ 1.5

spray/spreʸ/ 3.2

stadium/'steʸdiʸəm/ 2.2

stage/steʸdʒ/ 2.4

stale/steʸl/ 1.8

star/star/ 2.6, 3.10

stationery store/ 'steʸʃə,nɛriʸ stɔr/ 3.4

stay at home/,steʸ ət 'hoʷm/ 2.4

steak/steʸk/ 1.6

stereo/'stɛriʸ,oʷ/ 1.2

stick/stɪk/ 3.3

stir/stɜr/ 1.6

stool/stuʷl/ 1.2

store/stɔr/ 3.2

story (account of events) /'stɔriʸ/ 2.9

story (of a building) /'stɔriʸ/ 1.1

stove/stoʷv/ 1.6

straw/strɔ/ 1.7

strawberry/'strɔ,bɛriʸ/ 1.6

string/strɪŋ/ 3.3

striped/straɪpt/ 1.10

student/'stuʷdnt/ 3.6

study/'stʌdiʸ/ 3.6

stunt man/woman/'stʌnt ,mæn,-wʊmən/ 2.6

stylish/'staɪlɪʃ/ 1.10

suit/suʷt/ 1.9

supermarket /'suʷpər,markɪt/ 3.4

sweater/'swɛtər/ 1.9

sweep/swiʸp/ 1.5

swimming/'swɪmɪŋ/ 2.1

switch/swɪtʃ/ 1.2

table/'teʸbəl/ 1.2

tablecloth/'teʸbəl,klɔθ/ 1.7

table tennis/'teʸbəl ,tɛnɪs/ 2.1

tackle/'tækəl/ 2.2

take a bath/a shower/,teʸk ə 'bæθ, ə 'ʃaʊər/ 1.4

take a bite/,teʸk ə 'baɪt/ 1.7

take a test/an exam/,teʸk ə 'tɛst, ən ɪg'zæm/ 3.6

take a trip/,teʸk ə 'trɪp/ 2.4

take notes/,teʸk 'noʷts/ 3.6

talk show/'tɔk ʃoʷ/ 2.8

tax/tæks/ 3.5

teacher/'tiʸʃər/ 3.1

tease/tiʸz/ 2.5

television/'tɛlə,vɪʒən/ 1.2

television personality /'tɛlə,vɪʒən pərsə'nælətiʸ/ 2.6

tell a joke/,tɛl ə 'dʒoʷk/ 2.5

tell a riddle/,tɛl ə 'rɪdl/ 2.5

tennis/'tɛnɪs/ 2.1

tennis shoes/'tɛnɪs ʃuz/ 1.9

test/tɛst/ 3.6

textbook/'tɛkstbʊk/ 2.9

theater/'θiʸətər/ 2.4

threaten/'θrɛtn/ 2.10

throat/θroʷt/ 3.7

throw/θroʷ/ 2.2

tie n/taɪ/ 1.9

tie v/taɪ/ 3.3

tighten/'taɪtn/ 3.3

tight-fitting/,taɪt 'fɪtɪŋ/ 1.10

tired/taɪərd/ 1.3

title/'taɪtl/ 2.9

toothbrush/'tuʷθbrʌʃ/ 1.4

toothpaste/'tuʷθpeʸst/ 1.4

tournament/'tʊərnəmənt/ 2.2

towel/'taʊəl/ 1.4

track and field/træk ən fiʸld/ 2.1

tractor/'træktər/ 3.2

traditional/trə'dɪʃənəl/ 1.10

trial/'traɪəl/ 3.8

trip/trɪp/ 2.4

trumpet/'trʌmpɪt/ 2.7

T-shirt/'tiʸ ʃɜrt/ 1.9

tune/tuʷn/ 2.7

turkey/'tɜrkiʸ/ 1.6

turn sour/tɜrn 'saʊər/ 1.8

turtle neck/'tɜrtl ,nɛk/ 1.10

umpire/'ʌmpaɪər/ 2.2

unconsciousness /,ʌn'kanʃəsnɪs/ 1.3

underwear/'ʌndər,wɛər/ 1.9

unemployed/,ʌnɪm'plɔɪd/ 3.1

unfashionable /ʌn'fæʃənəbəl/ 1.10

universe/'yuʷnə,vɜrs/ 3.10

university/,yuʷnə'vɜrsətiʸ/ 3.6

unskilled/ʌn'skɪld/ 3.1

upstairs/,ʌp'stɛərz/ 1.1

vacuum v/'vækyuʷm/ 1.5

vacuum cleaner/'vækyuʷm ,kliʸnər/ 1.5

veal/viʸl/ 1.6

verdict/'vɜrdɪkt/ 3.8

vineyard/'vɪnyərd/ 3.2

violin/,vaɪə'lɪn/ 2.7

V-neck/'viʸ nɛk/ 1.10

volleyball/'valiʸ,bɔl/ 2.1

vomit/'vamɪt/ 3.7

vote/voʷt/ 3.9

voter/'voʷtər/ 3.9

wages/'weʸdʒɪz/ 3.5

waiter/'weʸtər/ 2.4

wake up/,weʸk 'ʌp/ 1.3

walk n/wɔk/ 2.4

walk (in front of a house) /wɔk/ 1.1

wall/wɔl/ 1.1

wardrobe/'wɔrdroʷb/ 1.2

warn/wɔrn/ 2.10

wash/waʃ/ 1.4

washing machine/'waʃɪŋ mə,ʃiʸn/ 1.5

water v/'wɔtər/ 3.2

weightlifting/'weʸt lɪftɪŋ/ 2.1

wheat/wiʸt/ 3.2

whisper/'wɪspər/ 2.10

white-collar/,waɪt 'kalər/ 3.1

wholesale price/'hoʷlseʸl praɪs/ 3.4

window/'wɪndoʷ/ 1.1

window-shopping/'wɪndoʷ ,ʃapɪŋ/ 2.4

windsurfing/'wɪnd,sɜrfɪŋ/ 2.1

wipe/waɪp/ 1.5

wire/waɪər/ 3.3

witness/'wɪtnɪs/ 3.8

witty/'wɪtiʸ/ 2.5

worth, be/wɜrθ/ 3.5

wound/wuʷnd/ 3.7

wrench/rɛntʃ/ 3.3

wrestling/'rɛsəlɪŋ/ 2.1

zoo/zuʷ/ 2.4

Key

Unit 1.1

Exercise 1

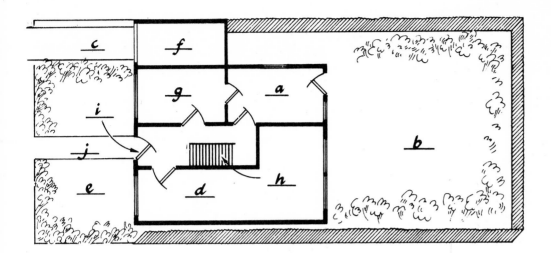

Exercise 2

1) e   2) h   3) b   4) g   5) f   6) a   7) d   8) c

Exercise 3

1) stairs — the other three are the sides of a room
2) roof — the other three are parts of a heating system
3) garage — the other three are rooms inside a house
4) wall — the other three are openings
5) story — the other three are specific areas in a house
6) walk — the other three are vertical structures

Just for fun

There are various possible answers to this exercise.

Unit 1.2

Exercise 1

The following do not exist in the 25th century:

1) **books** (the child says "what are those things . . . are they books?" — the child had heard of books but had never seen any before.)   2) **coffee** (the guide says it was made illegal 250 years ago)   3 **televisions** (the child says "What's that box?")   7) **records** (the guide has to explain what they are)   10) **sofas** (the guide explains what they are)
13) **cigarettes** (same as for coffee above)   15) **Mickey Mouse movies**

Exercise 2

1) g   2) d   3) h   4) a   5) f   6) b   7) c   8) e

Exercise 3

1) shelf   2) stereo   3) coffee table   4) ashtray   5) cassette player
6) compact disc player

Dictionary work

to sit on	**to put things in**	**to walk on**
a deckchair	a closet	a rug
a bench	a chest of drawers	a mat
a stool	a wardrobe	a carpet
a cushion	a cabinet	linoleum

Unit 1.3

Exercise 1

1 1) pillow   2) sheet   3) mattress   4) pajamas   5) blanket
2 Diagram 4 shows a normal night's sleep.

Exercise 2

1) d   2) f   3) b   4) c   5) g   6) a   7) e

Exercise 3

1) e   2) f   3) d   4) b   5) a   6) c

Just for fun

There are various possible answers to this exercise.

Unit 1.4

Exercise 1

1 Nowadays most homes have bathrooms.
2 In the past most people never brushed their teeth.
3 Nowadays most people wash every day.
4 In the past most people didn't use soap.
5 In the past most kings and queens of Europe didn't take baths.
6 Nowadays most people believe that it is important to be clean.
7 In the past most people needed to wear perfume.

Exercise 2

1) toothbrush used for brushing your teeth   2) soap used for washing yourself   3) towel used for drying yourself   4) bath used for taking a bath

Exercise 3

1) c   2) a   3) d   4) e   5) f   6) b

Dictionary work

1) g   2) a   3) d   4) c   5) b   6) e   7) f

Unit 1.5

Exercise 1

1) e   2) b   3) d   4) g   5) c   6) a   7) f

Exercise 2

1 spotless is almost opposite in meaning to filthy
2 dirty is almost opposite in meaning to clean
3 neat is almost opposite in meaning to messy
4 spotless means very very clean
5 filthy means very very dirty

Exercise 3

1) d   2) a   3) h   4) i   5) b   6) g   7) c   8) f   9) e

Just for fun

There are various possible answers to this exercise.

Test yourself 1

1) armchair   2) garage   3) ceiling   4) spotless   5) toothpaste   6) polish
7) cushion   8) blanket   9) perfume   10) filthy   11) hall   12) mattress
13) neat   14) towel   15) iron   16) nightmare   17) curtains   18) dishwasher
19) soap   20) roof   21) exhausted   22) drowsy/sleepy   23) switch
24) make-up   25) desk

Unit 1.6

Exercise 1

1) fried   2) scrambled   3) boiled   4) baked   5) egg salad

Exercise 2

1) oven   2) knife   3) frying pan   4) stove   5) spoon   6) saucepan   7) knife
8) spoon   9) knife

Exercise 3

1) d, f   2) a   3) a, g   4) e   5) d, f   6) a, c, g   7) a, b, e   8) a, b, c, g

Dictionary work

__M__ sausage	__M__ ham	__F__ grape	__V__ pea	__V__ bean
__F__ pineapple	__V__ celery	__M__ lamb	__V__ cabbage	__M__ beef
__F__ strawberry	__M__ steak	__F__ peach	__V__ spinach	__F__ avocado
__M__ turkey	__M__ veal	__F__ pear	__V__ cucumber	__F__ plum

Unit 1.7

Exercise 1

a) 4   b) 3   c) 9   d) 7   e) 1

Exercise 2

1) e   2) k   3) a   4) h   5) j   6) b   7) l   8) i   9) d   10) c   11) g   12) f

Just for fun

There are various possible answers to this exercise.

Unit 1.8

Exercise 1

1) bad   2) thousands   3) nineteenth   4) fresh   5) jars   6) metal   7) refrigerator   8) sour   9) rot
10) frozen

Exercise 2

sour	stale	rotten	
1 cream	3 cake	5 tomatoes	7 ham
2 milk	4 cookies	6 bananas	8 chicken

Exercise 3

1) f   2) e   3) a   4) c   5) h   6) b   7) d   8) g

Dictionary work

1) i   2) c   3) d   4) j   5) h   6) g   7) a   8) f   9) l   10) e   11) b   12) k

Unit 1.9

Exercise 1

1) T   2) F   3) T   4) F   5) F   6) T

Exercise 2

1) glove   2) pants   3) hat   4) boot   5) jacket   6) sock

Exercise 3

Chart 1

	above waist	below waist	above and below
1 jeans		X	
2 suit			X
3 dress			X
4 tie	X		
5 shorts		X	
6 scarf	X		
7 skirt		X	
8 underwear			X
9 shirt	X		

Chart 2

	women only	both men and women
1 T-shirt		X
2 underwear		X
3 jeans		X
4 blouse	X	
5 dress	X	
6 boots		X
7 jacket		X
8 gloves		X
9 skirt	X	

Just for fun

There are various possible answers to this exercise. Here is one possible set of answers.

1) shirt — the other three come in pairs
2) socks — the other three go over the legs not on your feet
3) underwear — the other three can usually be seen when you wear them
4) tie — the other three are usually worn to keep you warm
5) T-shirt — the other three are usually worn on more formal occasions

Unit 1.10

Exercise 1

1) b   2) b   3) a   4) a   5) b

Exercise 2

modern	old
in style	old-fashioned
stylish	conservative
popular	out-dated
in	out of style

Exercise 3

1) traditional   2) unfashionable   3) stylish   4) baggy

Dictionary work

1) j   2) l   3) d   4) k   5) b   6) a   7) h   8) e   9) i   10) c   11) g   12) f

Test yourself 2

1) stylish   2) boils   3) chew   4) tie   5) old-fashioned   6) raw   7) stir/pour   8) lick   9) style
10) stale   11) suit   12) ham   13) fashionable   14) box   15) napkins   16) hat   17) frozen
18) melt   19) sour   20) jar   21) dress   22) striped   23) oven   24) plate   25) boots

Unit 2.1

Exercise 1

1) 1896, Athens   2) 1936, Berlin   3) 1904, St. Louis   4) 1988, Seoul   5) 1964, Tokyo   6) 1896, Athens
7) 1908, London   8) 1964, Tokyo   9) 1984, Los Angeles

Exercise 2

sports played in teams	sports that can be played against one other person	sports that can be played alone
volleyball	judo	sailing
handball	boxing	golf
soccer	table tennis	swimming
basketball	tennis	cycling

Exercise 3

1) weightlifting   2) horseback riding   3) shooting   4) gymnastics   5) rowing   6) football

Just for fun

There are various possible answers to this exercise. Here is one possible set of answers.

1) tennis — all the others are team sports
2) volleyball — the other three involve fighting
3) table tennis — the other three you can do alone
4) basketball — in the other three you have to get the ball over a net
5) soccer — to do the other three you need some sort of bat or club
6) swimming— to do the other three you need some sort of boat or watercraft

Unit 2.2

Exercise 1
1) OK   2) Not OK   3) OK   4) Not OK

Exercise 2
1) f   2) h   3) d   4) b   5) e   ∂) a   7) g   8) c

Exercise 3
1) b, e, f, g   2) a, c, d   3) b, g   4) e, g   5) a, c, f   6) b, e   7) d   8) b, g

Dictionary work
1) g   2) d   3) b   4) f   5) a   6) c   7) h   8) e

Unit 2.3

Exercise 1
1) party   2) dance   3) enjoying   4) invited   5) friend   6) celebrate   7) fun   8) different   9) boring
10) crazy   11) cake   12) mother

Exercise 2
1) D   2) S   3) S   4) D   5) S   6) D   7) S   8) D   9) S   10) D

Just for fun
There are various possible answers to this exercise.

Unit 2.4

Exercise 1
1) i   2) f   3) d   4) a   5) j   6) g   7) b   8) h   9) c   10) e

Exercise 2
1) to a   2) 0   3) a   4) 0   5) for a   6) a   7) to the   8) to   9) the   10) at

Exercise 3

1) d   2) f   3) a   4) e   5) c   6) b

Dictionary work

1) i   2) f   3) j   4) c   5) b   6) a   7) g   8) d   9) h   10) e

Unit 2.5

Answers to riddles: 1) table   2) umbrella   3) tomorrow

Exercise 1

1) riddles   2) amusing   3) joke   4) witty   5) true   6) kidding   7) friendly   8) silly

Exercise 2

1) A   2) A   3) B   4) B   5) A   6) B

Exercise 3

1) c   2) d   3) b   4) a   5) e

Just for fun
You tell a joke!

Test yourself 3

1) tease   2) sightseeing   3) stay   4) scored   5) stage   6) invite   7) kidding   8) weightlifting
9) tournament   10) joke   11) basketball   12) trip   13) presents   14) witty/funny   15) net
16) enjoy   17) sailing   18) celebrate   19) amusing   20) referee   21) museum   22) shoot
23) boring   24) gymnastics   25) catch

Unit 2.6

Exercise 1

1) T   2) T   3) T   4) F   5) F   6) F   7) T   8) F

Exercise 2

1) clown   2) movie director   3) actress   4) magician   5) stunt man

Exercise 3

1) d   2) c   3) g   4) f   5) b   6) a   7) e

Just for fun
There are various possible answers to this exercise.

Unit 2.7

Exercise 1

1) c   2) a   3) e   4) f   5) d   6) b

Exercise 2

1) group *or* 2) band   3) melody *or* 4) tune   5) rhythm *or* 6) beat

Exercise 3

	rock 'n' roll	punk rock	folk	reggae	jazz	classical
1 often played by a big orchestra in a concert hall						X
2 often played by young people with guitars in a group	X	X	X	X		
3 often played by young people with brightly colored hair		X				
4 often simple tunes which are popular for a short time	X	X				
5 music coming originally from Afro-American musicians					X	
6 music of a specific region, popular for a very long time			X			
7 music with a strong regular rhythm, originally from Jamaica				X		
8 music which is popular for dancing in rock clubs	X	X		X		
9 often played freely, not following written music					X	

Dictionary work
1) e   2) d   3) f   4) b   5) c   6) a   7) h   8) g

Unit 2.8

Exercise 1
1) a   2) d   3) c   4) c   5) a   6) b   7) a   8) c

Exercise 2
1) i   2) d   3) f   4) g   5) a   6) e   7) c   8) j   9) b   10) h

Just for fun
Design your own evening of television.

Unit 2.9

Exercise 1
1) b   2) b   3) a   4) a   5) c

Exercise 2
fiction: novel, short story, play, poem
non-fiction: atlas, textbook, dictionary, encyclopedia

Exercise 3
1) f   2) c   3) e   4) i   5) a   6) g   7) h   8) d   9) b

Dictionary work
1) T   2) N   3) T   4) N   5) T   6) N   7) N   8) N   9) T   10) T   11) N   12) T

Unit 2.10

Exercise 1
1) b   2) c   3) b   4) c

Exercise 2
1) e   2) g   3) b   4) f   5) j   6) a   7) h   8) i   9) c   10) d

Dictionary work
1) i   2) f   3) d   4) b   5) l   6) g   7) e   8) k   9) h   10) a   11) j   12) c

Test yourself 4

1) classical   2) comedians   3) news   4) advise   5) chapter   6) channels   7) rock   8) glossary
9) actress   10) speech   11) drums   12) magicians   13) headline   14) series   15) mumble
16) movie director   17) poems   18) documentary   19) beat   20) whisper   21) clowns   22) group
23) chat   24) magazine   25) advertisements

Unit 3.1

Exercise 1

	Martha	George	Billy	No one
1 Who had a white-collar job for a while?		X		
2 Who works in a profession?	X			
3 Who wanted to become a secretary?				X
4 Who is unemployed at the moment?				X
5 Who is an unskilled worker?			X	
6 Who was a successful salesperson?		X		
7 Who wanted a different career as a child?	X			
8 Who married the boss?				X
9 Who has no career?			X	
10 Who was out of work for a while?			X	

Exercise 2

1) blue-collar worker is similar in meaning to factory worker
2) unemployed is similar in meaning to out of work
3) boss is similar in meaning to manager
4) office worker is similar in meaning to white-collar worker

Exercise 3

	professional worker	white-collar worker	skilled worker
1 engineer	X		
2 secretary		X	
3 bank teller		X	
4 architect	X		
5 teacher	X		
6 mechanic			X
7 lawyer	X		
8 computer repair person			X
9 office manager		X	
10 hairdresser			X

Just for fun

There are various possible answers to this exercise.

92

Unit 3.2

Exercise 1

	spring	summer	fall	winter
1 The fields are planted.	X			
2 The fruit is picked.			X	
3 The crops are sprayed.		X		
4 The corn is reaped.			X	
5 The fields are planned.				X
6 The wood is chopped.				X
7 The crops are stored in the barns.				X
8 The fields are plowed.	X			
9 The fields are watered.		X		
10 The fields are fertilized.	X			

Exercise 2

1) b 2) f 3) e 4) g 5) a 6) d 7) c

Exercise 3

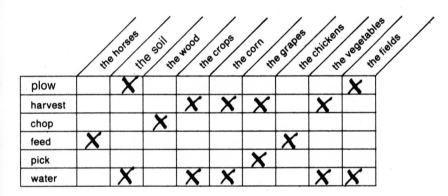

	the horses	the soil	the wood	the crops	the corn	the grapes	the chickens	the vegetables	the fields
plow		X							X
harvest				X	X	X		X	
chop			X						
feed	X						X		
pick					X				
water		X		X	X			X	X

Dictionary work

1) j 2) h 3) e 4) a 5) k 6) c 7) b 8) l 9) f 10) i 11) g 12) d

Unit 3.3

Exercise 1

a) 4 b) 3 c) 5 d) 6 e) 2 f) 1

Exercise 2

tools: hammer, wrench, saw, screwdriver
things used with tools: screw, nail, glue, bolt

Exercise 3

1) d 2) a 3) f 4) e 5) b 6) c

Just for fun

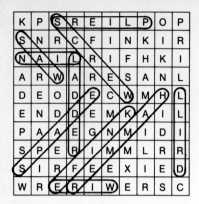

Unit 3.4

Exercise 1

1) F   2) T   3) T   4) T   5) F   6) F   7) T   8) F   9) F   10) T

Exercise 2

1) S   2) S   3) D   4) D   5) S   6) D

Exercise 3

1) e   2) a   3) d   4) g   5) b   6) c   7) f

Dictionary work

1) j   2) e   3) c   4) i   5) a   6) d   7) h   8) g   9) f   10) b

Unit 3.5

Exercise 1

1) e   2) g   3) h   4) c   5) a   6) d   7) b   8) f

Exercise 2

1) a   2) b   3) a   4) b   5) a

Exercise 3

In the United States and Great Britain, many people would like to ___*own*___ their own homes, but it is usually very difficult to ___*save*___ enough money. Most people ___*spend*___ as much as they ___*earn*___ each month. But if you can't ___*afford*___ to buy a house, often you can get a bank to ___*lend*___ you most of the money to buy one. The bank knows that a house is a very good place for you to ___*invest*___ your money. A few years after you buy it, a house is usually ___*worth*___ much more than it originally ___*cost*___ you, so you can ___*sell*___ it for a big profit.

Dictionary work

1) f   2) c   3) a   4) i   5) d   6) b   7) e   8) g   9) j   10) h

Test yourself 5

1) afford   2) harvest   3) profession   4) unskilled   5) department   6) boss   7) check   8) cattle
9) discount   10) screwdriver   11) salesperson   12) saw   13) planted   14) bargain   15) taxes
16) nails   17) tractor   18) lend   19) glue   20) unemployed   21) ladder   22) pick   23) receipt
24) owe   25) interest

Unit 3.6

Exercise 1

1) b   2) c   3) b   4) a   5) a   6) c

Exercise 2

place for learning	person who studies	something produced by a student
college	freshman	essay
elementary school	senior	homework
university	student	notes

Exercise 3

1) c, a, b   2) c, b, a   3) b, a, c   4) b, c, a   5) a, b, c

Just for fun

There are various possible answers to this exercise.

Unit 3.7

Exercise 1

1) b   2) d   3) a   4) c

Exercise 2

1) c   2) g   3) b   4) f   5) d   6) a   7) e

Exercise 3

1) e   2) d   3) c   4) f   5) a   6) b

Just for fun

There are various possible answers to this exercise.

Unit 3.8

Exercise 1

More than one answer is possible, but these are the suggested answers.

1) How old is Mullins?
2) When did the trial begin?
3) How did Mullins kill his wife?
4) Who gave evidence at the trial?
5) How long will Mullins have to stay in prison?
6) When will Mullins be released from prison?

Exercise 2

1) d   2) a   3) b   4) c

Exercise 3

1) e   2) b   3) f   4) i   5) j   6) k   7) c   8) a   9) h   10) d   11) g

Dictionary work

1) e   2) h   3) g   4) f   5) d   6) a   7) b   8) c

Unit 3.9

Exercise 1

1) b   2) c   3) c   4) c

Exercise 2

1) d   2) f   3) e   4) a   5) c   6) h   7) b   8) g

Exercise 3

1 (N) politics
2 (V) vote
3 (V) govern   4 (N) government
5 (V) elect   6 (A) presidential   7 (N) election
8 (N) politician   9 (A) political

Dictionary work

1) republic   2) political   3) industrial   4) president   5) politician   6) society
7) conservative   8) democracy   9) social   10) ambassador   11) democratic
12) economy   13) politics   14) industry   15) economic

Unit 3.10

Exercise 1

1) F   2) T   3) F   4) T   5) T   6) F   7) F

Exercise 2

1) astronaut   2) be launched   3) orbit

Exercise 3

1) g   2) d   3) c   4) f   5) e   6) a   7) b

Just for fun

1) e   2) c   3) a   4) f   5) b   6) d   7) g   8) i   9) h

Test yourself 6

1) astronaut   2) failed   3) voted   4) planet   5) fever   6) headache
7) prison   8) kidnapping   9) shuttle   10) college   11) moon   12) princesses
13) homework   14) cough   15) witness   16) democracy   17) economic   18) pain
19) students   20) hurt/ache   21) arrested   22) satellites   23) take   24) government
25) trial